The
Intimate
Marriage

To order additional copies of *The Intimate Marriage,*
by Alberta Mazat, call 1-800-765-6955.

Visit us at *www.reviewandherald.com* for information on
other Review and Herald products.

The Intimate Marriage

CONNECTING WITH THE ONE YOU LOVE

Alberta Mazat

REVIEW AND HERALD® PUBLISHING ASSOCIATION
HAGERSTOWN, MD 21740

This book was
Edited by Andy Nash
Copyedited by Delma Miller and James Cavil
Designed by Bill Kirstein
Electronic makeup by Shirley M. Bolivar
Cover illustration art by Janet Atkinson, stock illustration source
Typeset: 11/15 Garamond Light

PRINTED IN U.S.A.

05 04 03 02 01   5 4 3 2 1

R&H Cataloging Service

Mazat, Alberta, 1919-
    The intimate marriage: connecting with the one you love

    1. Intimacy (Psychology).   2. Marriage.   I. Title.

                306.81

ISBN 0-8280-1446-9

Dedicated to

My intimate other of 56 years
and our four children and their spouses—

Al and Jeanne
Jo Ann and Dick
Janie and Michael
Nancy and Jay

whom we consider to be
our dearest friends.

Acknowledgments

Thanks to all those who
helped the computer make some sense
(you know who you are)
and to editor
Jeannette Johnson, who was patient
when it didn't.

Contents

CHAPTER 1

Let's Begin!

One Year . . .

Judy and Jud had been married for one year. In spite of a few adjustment problems—well, actually, more than a few—they felt that they had a good marriage. They enjoyed doing things together, and they usually talked over situations when there seemed to be threatening differences. They felt good about the pleasure they had in lovemaking. This joyous experience of bonding, they had discovered, was so closely tied to their interpersonal harmony that they tried to remember to make their relationship a top priority. They seemed to have far fewer arguments and disagreements than many of their friends did. Yes, they were pretty pleased with their first year of marriage, and sometimes remarked that if things kept getting more wonderful—as Pastor Williams had suggested they could in his marriage homily—this first anniversary was a harbinger of many wonderful years to come.

Eight Years . . .

Mary Ann and Ken surveyed the family room discord as they waved goodbye to the last of the little partygoers. Jimmy had just celebrated his sixth birthday with 10 of his friends—what a mess! The game-playing, toy-trying 6-year-olds had been as good as game-playing, toy-trying 6-year-olds can be, and it had been very gratifying to see little Jimmy so excited and pleased with the whole event. He had even re-membered to thank his friends without being prompted—most of the time, anyway.

For a few minutes Mary Ann and Ken just sat there in the midst of the disorder and looked at each other with a weary sigh. "You know," said Ken, "I just re-alized that tomorrow is our eighth wedding anniver-sary. Can you believe how things have changed since our first years of marriage? Having Jimmy was a real blessing—but we have to admit it surely has changed our lives a lot."

"I won't disagree with that!" Mary Ann smiled as she caressed Ken's cheek. "Remember how we used to throw things into the back of the car and impul-sively take off for a weekend at the beach?"

"Mm—yeah, and I have such pleasant memories of sleeping late on Sunday mornings with no inter-ruptions and plenty of time to talk. I remember how we used to bring the Sunday paper into bed to read, and then get all tangled up in legs and arms and newsprint until we finally got so hungry we had to get up and fix breakfast together—or else take a quick trip to IHOP!"

Mary Ann turned pensive. "I really hope this doesn't mean that we are falling into the 'marriage trap.' I've read how some couples who have been married for a long time don't feel the same closeness as they did early in marriage. That couldn't happen to us, could it?"

Fifteen Years . . .

Alexa and Tim looked over their schedules. A fifteenth wedding anniversary should certainly carry some precedence.

"No," said Tim, "that's the day of the company picnic, and I'm in charge of arrangements. The boss made it rather clear that he hoped it would go smoother than it had last year."

"But then the next day," said Alexa, "is Timmy's playoff game, and we already missed the last one. How about the twentieth—that's just a week late."

"No," corrected Tim. "Sandy leaves for junior camp that day, and we promised to drive all her friends."

"Well," kidded Alexa, "maybe we could stop at some fast-food place on the way back."

Tim sighed. "Whoever wrote the book on marriage partners becoming more and more bonded, and more and more intimate, couldn't have had careers or kids."

Twenty-five Years . . .

Janice and Vic looked with great pleasure at their travel folder. This twenty-fifth anniversary was really going to happen. They were going to take a three-day cruise to a quiet island and stay for a week. It would be just like a second honeymoon! What a break they had gotten on the tickets through Vic's brother. They might be making payments for a few months, but it would be worth it—and they deserved it. Janice's parents were available if the children called from academy or college with any problems—though that was quite unlikely. Now for some quality time together.

Janice and Vic decided that, along with having fun, they were going to plan some quality time for sharing together. In a recent sermon their pastor had said that it was a good idea for couples to evaluate their marriages every now and then. He had even given them an inventory to help them explore their relationship spiritually and interpersonally. They could discuss what they wanted to happen in their marriage over the next 10 years. He had also given them some discussion guidelines, which Janice had carefully tucked in her Bible. This was really going to be meaningful. Along with their Bibles, she had packed *The Desire of Ages* for good measure.

But the strangest thing happened. Whenever they decided it was time to "talk," they got sidetracked. Had they remembered to send the check for the last car payment? Should they borrow money to have Penny's teeth straightened? Should the boys begin using their own money for the clothes they "have to have"?

With all these loose ends, Janice and Vic never did get around to discussing anything in-depth. When they did manage to look at the pastor's inventory, Vic remembered that he must call the head deacon as soon as they got home to report an uneven break on the church sidewalk. After all, they could be sued if someone fell . . .

And so it went—into the thirtieth, fortieth, and fiftieth anniversaries. Janice and Vic practically forgot how to talk and share at the "gut level." True intimacy had become a thing of the past.

દ⁂ દ⁂ દ⁂

Too many couples have found themselves at this same juncture in their marital odyssey. For some it's not distressing. For one reason or another, they had never really expected more than a relationship that just endured. The rut is so comfortable that they are willing to slog all the way to the New Jerusalem in marriages that hold few surprises and much mindless repetition.

Was this God's plan for this special Edenic gift of marriage—which was to be a foretaste of heaven itself? I agree with one of my favorite authors, Ellen White, when she says, "There is a serious lack of love's precious influence" in marriages.[1] When wives and husbands spend as much time contemplating how to "love and . . . be loved"[2] as they do running their households, furthering their careers, and even meeting their church's obligations, then we should be able to enjoy the kinds of marital unions that God designed to be a "lifelong blessing."[3]

With a deep desire for such Christian homes—and years of counseling couples who *want* to be closer—I am motivated to bring together these thoughts. My purpose is to explain the *total* spectrum of intimacy in marriage and to share some practical suggestions for drawing couples closer.

Once a book leaves the publishing house and enters the readers' hands, an author has little say in how it will be used. *But if I did,* it would be an earnest plea for husbands and wives to read this book together—or if it is read separately, to discuss it together. It could bring a whole new dimension to your intimacy.

[1] *The Adventist Home,* p. 109.
[2] *Patriarchs and Prophets,* p. 46.
[3] *The Adventist Home,* p. 110.

CHAPTER 2

The Essence of Intimacy

The word "intimacy" is not unfamiliar, yet we have difficulty capturing its essence. Sometimes it is taken to mean frequency of contact with a person, or being in close bodily proximity to another. But this definition could include a grocery checkout person or even a huddle of football players. Obviously, neither of these would qualify as an intimate relationship. Most often the term is taken to identify sexual contact with another person. But sexuality and intimacy are not the same thing. Sex is more accessible, usually less time-consuming, and can be devoid of emotional closeness or commitment—qualities that make intimacy desirable and fulfilling.

Intimacy will be defined here as a feeling of warmth and closeness. It implies an affinity, a feeling of rapport. It is an experience of oneness with a person with whom we want to share how we feel and think. In a relationship with an intimate other, our dreams, values, goals, joys, and disappointments will be mutually disclosed in a protected atmosphere.

We were created with a deep need for love and companionship. God designed Eve and Adam with the capacity to love and be loved. They were to be companions who would be one in "love and sympathy."[1] This was not something self-generated but something they were given, along with other God-planted capabilities. Love is experienced through our senses, and in an intimate relationship each partner has the privilege—and yes, the responsibility—of learning how to use these capabilities to demonstrate God's plan for an intimate marriage.

Couples who marry want more than a common address; they want total intimacy. They hope to find acceptance, understanding, and love. They look forward to an inner warmth, a closeness that distinguishes their relationship from every other relationship they have. But even though marriage provides the very best setting, intimacy is not the automatic, instantaneous, mystical result of marriage. It is the by-product of love, understanding, knowledge, and time.

It would be simpler, of course, if a guarantee of intimacy in its various dimensions came attached to the marriage certificate. But it would not be as appreciated or as growth-producing. Actually, that important piece of paper should be marked, "This product is perishable; handle with care." Though marriage can be as durable as the strongest steel when cherished and nurtured, it is as fragile as a gossamer thread when neglected or misused. Genuine intimacy is created and endures only when both members of the marriage partnership are eager and willing to be part of a loving relationship to which they pledge continuing effort.

Perhaps when we can put to rest the false notion that being *really* in love translates into a good marriage, more engaged couples will realize that premarital counseling is an important preparation for an intimate marriage. They will understand why most churches are now making this type of counseling obligatory for the couple wishing to be married by a minister in that church. This is not the time to scurry around finding a different pastor or church. What they can learn through premarital counseling will give them a head start in uniting their separate lives into a new relationship.

It is of utmost importance for a man and woman to spend their courtship time getting acquainted with each other's minds and hearts. This is much more important than learning about physical body responses. God designed physical intimacy to *follow* emotional, intellectual, and spiritual intimacy. It's His gift for the wedding day.

Some couples look to marriage to *give* them love, affection, and happiness. Actually, that is not the role of marriage. Each partner must *bring into* the marriage the ability to give love and affection—and the habit of happiness. When these elements join together in the advantageous setting that marriage can provide, a wondrous intimacy can result.

Does it sound difficult, illusive, even unlikely to achieve? The good news is that many couples have made and are continuing to make that effort and are finding great joy in the doing. They would want me to tell you that experiencing intimacy in its total dimension is the most satisfying and fulfilling relationship possible. God designed it to be that way, and He doesn't make mistakes.

Intimacy was not new to the universe. The Father and Son had always been closely united. From eternity they had been one in purpose, harmony, and character.[2] Jesus refers to this close relationship in a conversation with His Father: "All I have is yours, and all you have is mine. . . . We are one" (John 17:10, 11, NIV). And He looked ahead with longing to the time when "they [the disciples] may be one as we are one: I in them and you in me" (verses 22, 23, NIV).

I like to try to fathom the sense of joy that existed in Their relationship. A glimpse of this is portrayed in Proverbs 8:29, 30: "He marked out the foundations of the earth. Then I was the craftsman at his side. I was filled with delight day after day, rejoicing always in his presence" (NIV). What a charming picture of Their togetherness! I believe that this is the intimacy we are invited to experience with our Creator. This is what He has bequeathed to us as we enter marriage. God has often used marriage as a symbol of His love for us (see Eph. 5:21-33). Apparently this is a heritage He wishes us to keep before us as we blend our lives in marriage.

Adam enjoyed "face-to-face, heart-to-heart communion with his Maker" that would have gone on forever "had he remained loyal to God."[3] There can be no doubt that intimacy was part of God's plan for His creation.

We are now going to discuss some dimensions of this intimacy. Let us realize before we begin that intimacy cannot really be separated into mutually exclusive categories in practice. But for ease of discussion, some students of intimacy have separated it into a number of categories, which they describe as "facets of a diamond." In their book *The Intimate Marriage* Howard and Charlotte Clinebell list these intimacies: sexual intimacy, emotional intimacy, intellectual intimacy, aesthetic intimacy, creative intimacy, recreational intimacy, work intimacy, crisis intimacy, conflict intimacy, commitment intimacy, spiritual intimacy, and communication intimacy.

In this book I have chosen to cover four of these areas, which I believe encompass the others. These four are the emotional, intellectual, physical, and spiritual intimacies. I list them alphabetically to avoid impression that they have been selected hierarchically! But let me reiterate that while we are looking at them separately, each will constantly impinge upon the others in subtle and powerful ways.

Before we do this, we are going to take an interesting side trip.

---

[1] *Patriarchs and Prophets,* p. 46.
[2] *The Great Controversy,* p. 493.
[3] *Education,* p. 15.

CHAPTER 3

Biblical Examples of Intimacy

We tend to think of the persons in Scripture as "Bible characters from long, long ago" rather than flesh-and-blood persons such as we are. We find it difficult to picture them with emotions, minds, and hearts that worked the same as ours do now. But we have all been made in God's image. In spite of differences in time, place, and culture, we should be able to identify with them as we read their stories, listen to their conversations, and observe their actions. They have something to reveal to us about the four intimacies we will study in future chapters.

Emotional Intimacy

Of the many wonderful examples of emotional intimates, we will look at two. In 1 Samuel we meet two dear and yet unlikely friends, David and Jonathan—one an unsophisticated country boy, the other a city prince. Amazingly, their relationship endured even through a reversal of roles. Jonathan came to acknowledge David as successor to his father, King Saul.

Their friendship transcended these circumstances, and their love and devotion to each other grew until it was described in these graphic terms: "Their souls were knit together" (see 1 Sam. 18:1). That is a very strong bond! One can unravel a knit garment, but it is nearly impossible to tear it apart.

We can only imagine all the things that they discussed together. Jonathan must have been thrilled as David told of keeping wild animals from ravaging his flock. Perhaps David was fascinated by Jonathan's perspective on his father's call to the kingship of Israel. He may have sympathized upon hearing how Jonathan's father had changed over the years—the fits of anger that could be soothed only by David's harp.

We can even imagine them swapping skills—one in slingshot marksmanship, the other in bow and arrow. We wonder if David needed reassurance from Jonathan that he wasn't too disappointed in being overlooked for the kingship. We know only that in spite of all these circumstances, they were deeply devoted to each other.

Their time together was interrupted by King Saul's intent to kill David. Loyal Jonathan helped plan David's successful escape. Their last recorded meeting touches us deeply. These two dear friends, a prince and a future king, not ashamed to show their emotions, "kissed each other and wept together" (1 Sam. 20:41, NIV). We could have wished for a happier ending, but let us not underestimate the effect of this beautiful friendship and the way it enriched both of their lives. Emotional intimacy does that wherever it is cultivated. Certainly it is the Creator's will that we learn to use this gift to bless others and to make our own lives fuller—an important aspect of a marital relationship.

We find another example of emotional intimacy in a young girl and an older woman. An unlikely pairing, but God knew what a blessing they could be to each other. Young Mary had just been given the unbelievable news that she was to become a mother. Naturally she was "greatly troubled" and wondering what she should do, whom she should turn to. In great kindness her messenger angel, Gabriel, gave immediate help in the form of an announcement of another pregnancy—a most remarkable one. Mary's elderly relative, Elisabeth, was also with child. Elisabeth? At her age? What was God up to?

Mary lost no time, immediately tramping over the Judean hills to Elisabeth's home. Surely with every step she became more eager to get some answers. And what an emotional welcome she received! In the expression of their joy at being together under the circumstances, they broke into poetry so beautiful that many generations continue to enjoy it. Can't you just see them embracing, rejoicing, and, yes, crying? Then came the dialogue of questions and answers . . .

What did your angel look like? . . . Tell me again exactly what your husband said. . . . How are your parents taking all this? . . . When did you start feeling pregnant? . . . What are your symptoms? . . . Tell me again what the angel said you should name your baby. . . . Oh, Mary, do you suppose this will truly be the Messiah?

These two remarkable women were different in so many ways, and yet they had so much in common. Perhaps sometimes these unusual circumstances frightened them and they wished for more "normal" pregnancies, but they must have been a great comfort to each other. For three months they talked, rejoiced, puzzled, maybe speculated—and then started all over again.

And they did have a little "advantage": Zechariah could not interrupt them. He couldn't say, "Won't you two women rest from your talking for a few moments? Will you never run out of questions?" Perhaps this was no coincidence. Any woman who has ever been pregnant can understand their need to disclose feelings, to share and gather support for the days ahead. And only God knew what was in the future for these two exceptional women.

No doubt they stored in their minds bits of their conversations, sentences from their prayers, and lyrics from the songs of rejoicing that would come back to them in the dark days ahead. That is one of the remarkable things about an intimate relationship—you can relive it when you most need it.

Intellectual Intimacy

At first glance this heading seems to be a contradiction. How can you combine the "head stuff" with the "heart stuff"? While people often feel close to someone who thinks as they do, who shares the same ideas, they might find it difficult to feel close to someone who disagrees with them.

Let us look at a pair of time-proven friends whose story we find in Acts. Paul and Barnabas met under circumstances that did not look promising for a close, trusting relationship on any dimension. But friendship took root and continued to grow. They even became traveling companions—which can add stress to any relationship. But they had a common purpose.

We can imagine them traveling the dusty roads, discussing the theological issues of the day. They didn't always agree—certainly not about the young intern Mark. Yet they were apparently able to rise above disagreements to preserve their relationship.

How much they endured together—from threats of stoning to being feted as gods. Can't you imagine them discussing these different receptions and trying to understand what made the difference? Did they wonder out loud what would have happened if they had used a different approach? Did they compliment each other on the handling of a question, a slur, or a dispute? Did they generally encourage and pray for each other? Knowing Paul and Barnabas as we do, we can't imagine either one of them ridiculing, rudely contradicting, or belittling the other—their intellectual intimacy would not have survived under those circumstances. Nor will ours.

These two stalwarts are exemplars of intellectual intimacy. Paul could say of this friend, as he did of another friend, Timothy: "Your love has given me great joy and encouragement, because you, brother, have refreshed the hearts of the saints" (Philemon 7, NIV).

Physical Intimacy

Touching adds another dimension to intimacy. Right now we are not talking about sexual physicalness, although our culture has sometimes made it difficult to keep that separated from social or friendly touching. I am thinking now about the touching that adds to our quality of caring. Among these are touches of greeting, affirmation, congratulations, comforting, and parting.

The Bible was written in a culture in which touching was part of the social experience. In our Western world we often seem anxious about any kind of touching beyond the chaste handshake. We no doubt miss the warmth and validation that appropriate touching can provide. Reading Paul's reminder of the "holy kiss" and remembering Christ's ministry of gentle touches* does not allay our anxiety enough to make us fully comfortable with touching.

You no doubt have heard people say, "Once you start this touching, where is it going to end? Can't this sort of thing get out of hand?" Yes, it certainly can. But cold formality in our families and churches is *already* out of hand. Doesn't it seem reasonable that if we can trust the Holy Spirit to help us make vital decisions on church boards and constituency meetings, we can trust the Holy Spirit's guidance in appropriate touch?

The most personal and restricted physical intimacy, of course, is reserved for the marriage relationship. Scripture very clearly reports occasions when couples engaged in sexual intercourse. Sometimes it is spoken of as "knowing," which is such an appropriate term. It implies that their intimacy was total, not simply a physical blending. We read of Eve and Adam, Rebekah and Isaac, Hannah and Elkanah, and many others.

It is also interesting to note the not-so-positive terms for sexual intimacy. David "lay" with Bathsheba. Ruth "uncovered Boaz's feet." Abraham "went in unto" Hagar, as did Jacob to Bilhah. I believe that Scripture makes it very clear that God's choicest blessings are reserved for sexual intimacy within a marriage where love is present. This type of sexual relationship is a symbol of God's love for His church. It is exclusive, faithful, selfless, and joyful in each dimension of the relationship.

Spiritual Intimacy

I don't consider this a "fourth" in a series of intimacies, but rather one that undergirds and indwells the others. God provides a perfect model of engaging in intimacy with another. He demonstrates so many of the qualities of which intimacy is built. Let's consider two examples.

First, Moses—with whom God spoke face-to-face while lovingly protecting him from the full radiance of His glory and majesty. When God spoke to Moses, Moses listened well, carefully considering what He said. This is a prime prerequisite for building intimacy. Moses spent so much time with God that he knew Him well. He felt safe enough, close enough, to talk straight with God. Quite pointedly, Moses reminded God of His promises. He remonstrated with God and resisted some of His plans, even appearing to admonish Him. But God was not "turned off." He listened with understanding and considered where Moses was coming from. He did not desert His dear old intimate. Instead

He honored him by revealing His glory to him. That gives us a window into how God feels about His intimate friends.

David also shared an intimate relationship with God. He freely disclosed to Him his depressions, his elations, his anger, his feelings of revenge and sorrow, as well as his heartfelt repentance. God never gave up on him. Through all their years of association God called him a man after His own heart. I have asked myself, "What! That adulterer, that murderer, that vengeful fellow who was wildly elated at times and in the depths of despair at other times? This is the material for a spiritually intimate relationship? *This* David?"

And then I remind myself, "No, not *that* David! David the sincerely repentant one, David who knew how to rejoice in and praise his Friend, David who loved God's law and saw so much beauty in it, David who delighted in spending time in His presence— that David!

When we study these intimate relationships, God opens up great wells of love within us. Through Moses and David and Enoch and Mary and Martha and Paul, we can understand spiritual intimacy so much better.

---

* See *The Desire of Ages,* p. 516.

CHAPTER 4

The Development of Intimacy

Every couple has their own history, and most enjoy recalling how they met and the course of their romance. We can usually count on the wife to give a more detailed story, emphasizing the most romantic moments. Listeners are almost always interested in this recital, frequently prompting with questions and encouraging further details. We love happy endings. At weddings we like to picture the radiant couple drifting from a blissful honeymoon to a life of close encounters of the intimate kind.

But intimacy does not come ready-made. It's a process beginning with two persons who at one time didn't even know each other—and then move along the continuum. Couples who marry usually intend to be splendidly happy together for life. While some might marry for other reasons—career advancement, companionship, readily available sex, security—they still expect a reasonable amount of well-being.

We need to spend some time, then, exploring the development of intimacy in a relationship between a woman and a man. On the far left of this continuum we find the "separateness" of two persons, whom we will call Jack and Jill. This simply means that these two persons are completely noncognizant of each other. Very few married couples were "cradle-mates"; their awareness of each other came later.

Awareness

The first progress in the relationship will change this status to "awareness." This can happen in several ways. Jack and Jill may have seen each other in a public place, such as a college library, a church, their workplace, or some social event Either one may then have made an overture at that time (or later) of routine friendliness. Awareness may also have come through a formal introduction by a friend, relative, or coworker. In the case of our friends, a laboratory supervisor introduced them when Jill was added to the overworked staff at a university facility. In the past, both had experienced many such introductions in other settings, but these didn't develop any further. However, this incident did move Jack and Jill, if ever so slightly, toward the other end of the continuum. Forming an intimate relationship is certainly not instantaneous—and seldom even rapid. It is a process that needs time and attention.

Pause Here . . .

When we come to this place in a seminar, the couples are asked to spend a few moments recalling the first time they became aware of each other. The reaction is very interesting. At first the couple might hesitate self-consciously. But soon they're smiling and laughing, even cuddling. It's usually a pleasant experience. Recalling a shared history helps emphasize their togetherness.

If you are reading this book with your spouse,

why not spend a few moments doing the same thing? I realize that sharing can be scary when not done regularly. It is a learned skill. But give it a try. Take a few moments to share your first awareness of your wife or husband. Name one *positive* impression you had about the other. Can you remember some of your feelings? Did you have any idea that this would be the first step in a process that would end in marriage?

Chitchat

The next step on this continuum is "chitchat." Early conversations between Jack and Jill were brief and probably not profound. Generally, not knowing each other keeps initial conversation on rather inconsequential matters. People usually ask casual things, such as: Have you lived here long? Where did you go to high school? college? Is it really as windy in Nebraska as they say it is? Where is the best shopping area around here? Are you a baseball fan—will you be watching the Series? Which team are you cheering for?

Pause Here . . .

Time to stop and recall again. Do you remember some of the first things you talked about? Some people can give a very specific answer, which surprises their mate (who was perhaps more interested in the way her eyes sparkled or the cleft on his chin). These are fun things to know and to add to a couple's history.

Someone may be saying, "I chitchatted with a lot

of people. What's that got to do with anything?" Just this. For some reason, chitchatting with the person you eventually married was more pleasant than chitchatting with others. Chitchatting with others may have revealed a personality that was not easy to like or a language that turned you off or didn't interest you enough to spend much time with that person. You obviously enjoyed talking with your future spouse because you made more opportunities to do so.

Dating

The next step on the continuum is spending planned time together—dating. One of the chief ingredients in forming relationships is time. Without a time investment, intimacy could never be achieved.

On the other hand, spending time together might also demonstrate to one or the other—perhaps both—that their relationship might not be that desirable, after all. Samples? She talks too much. He's a bore. He picks his teeth. She's always fussing with her hair. They couldn't find anything in common. They had different ideals, values, goals, senses of humor. The list goes on.

Dating is a very valuable social form for these precise reasons—and usually one or two dates aren't enough. Being together under different circumstances will help each person know whether to continue or not.

Pause Here . . .

Take some time now to talk together about your very first dates—what you did, your response to the activity, and the reasons you decided to continue dating. Discuss some of your very favorite dates. This should be a fun activity. After all, if your dating had been a continuing disaster, you wouldn't be reading this book together.

By the way, dating is a very American custom. When the industrial evolution moved people from rural settings where families knew each other for several generations, young women and men needed a means to get acquainted with the opposite sex. Dating evolved. Originally, it was very protected, with insistence upon chaperones to accompany the young people and careful instructions as to activities and behaviors.

Deeper Sharing

As a couple spends more and more time together, they learn more about each other's emotions, thinking, and spiritual commitment. From talking about people, things, and daily events, they move to self-disclosures. It becomes more comfortable and natural to talk more openly about their families and significant things from the past. When we move to a deeper level of communication, we feel good about being able to share problems, issues, and ideas with someone who seems truly interested. We feel heard, validated, and important in the relationship. This will be one of the greatest assets of marriage—always having someone to listen, hear, and support. We like to think that this feeling of close communion will always be part of our relationship.

Pause Here . . .

When you were dating, what did you discuss with each other? What was it about your partner's ability to talk that made you realize she or he would be a valuable part of your life? Is there an aspect of this "sharing time" that you would like to see reactivated? Do you feel you were "better at it" earlier in your relationship than you are now? If so, why?

Touching

Something else happens when we begin to feel a closer tie with someone. There comes a desire to experience that person in another dimension as well—the dimension of touching. Some of our most treasured memories are that first time we held hands, that first hug, that first kiss. Sometimes couples can recall where and when. Can you?

Now that you are married, do you get as much of these three activities? Do you wish you would hold hands, hug, and kiss more often—not as a prelude for more intense lovemaking, but simply as freestanding demonstrations of affection?

Pause Here . . .

Talk about that for a moment or two—you may be surprised at your partner's response. Let me venture to guess: She would like more, while he may be satisfied but would be thinking more in terms of more lovemaking.

❧ ❧ ❧

Now back to the continuum and the "touching" phase of intimacy. When we were teens, our parents began to get a little edgy about our being physically close to our dates. Having been over the same road, they realize that this is a rather insistent and urgent desire to be close. They are concerned that hormones will overrule rational thinking. Sometimes the advice they give is somewhat long on what could result from "unbridled passion" (a favorite warning from *my* youth) and short on good reasons for using touch appropriately and in the proper time sequence.

Many marital therapists and youth workers have seen marriages flounder because couples did not spend enough time getting to know each other's emotions, ideas, values, and goals before they reached out physically. Let's face it! Compared to talking about in-laws, careers, money, household roles, and conflict resolution, having sex seems much more attractive. It is good to know that sexual problems arising from premature sexual expression can be worked through. Yet it would have been much easier to start sexual interaction right where God planned it—marriage. Sexuality does not benefit by practice before marriage. We will discuss the whole area of sexual intimacy in a later chapter.

Marriage

After dating, sharing, and touching on the road to intimacy, the couple is usually at the point of declaring their love, announcing their engagement, and making wedding plans. What an exciting time this is! We have all heard interesting and sometimes humorous stories of how the decision to marry came about—but none will be as exciting or as important as your story. Talk about the moment of your proposal.

Pause Here . . .

Stop for a moment and recall how you concluded that you were right for each other—and ready for marriage.

ᴂ   ᴂ   ᴂ

Whether it was a quiet ceremony with family only or a large wedding resplendent with attendants, flowers, and music, your wedding is unforgettable. Couples too need to relive this important milestone more often than they do.

Pause Here . . .

This may not be the opportune time to make an "event" out of it. But sometime soon (set the date now), get out the pictures, listen to the tapes, view the slides and video again, and listen to yourselves repeat your vows. Recall the specialness of meeting each other at the altar, of looking into each other's eyes during your vows. Parts of the wedding story will probably bring tears—and laughter (even though it might not have seemed funny at the time). Revel in your story.

❧ ❧ ❧

We have passed from first "awareness" to total intimacy—in which you can anticipate the total togetherness of each aspect of your relationship. The words of Ellen White, spoken at a wedding held in her home, seem particularly appropriate. She took the bride and groom by the hand and said, "Make God your counselor. Blend, blend together."[1] In her extensive work with others, she knew well the importance of forging and maintaining the closeness of intimacy in each aspect of their lives.

She also realized something else of crucial importance. In a written communication she said, "Let there be mutual love, mutual forbearance. Then marriage, instead of being the end of love, will be as it were the very beginning of love."[2] How timely this advice is to us in a day when nearly half of marriages end in divorce!

Love in marriage really can get better and better—it is a growing thing full of promise for happiness through the years. In other words, couples who do practice "mutual love" in all its dimensions should feel more and more involved in all the intimacies that make marriage so desirable.

This does not always seem to be the nature of things. With regularity, couples report to marriage counselors that they do *not* feel as close and don't have the same warmth in their relationship. They have not only stopped growing in their intimacy dimensions, but are even going backward. They are actually moving from the right to the left of the continuum.

Sure, they might still be involved in sexual intimacies, but it is more often a response to sexual stimuli and a desire for the "adrenaline rush" that accompanies intercourse than it is a deep desire to be part of each other's total being.

Backing up still further on the continuum: Their touching now is more often simply a prelude to a sexual experience. The touching, caressing, kissing, and holding they used to find so enjoyable before marriage is no longer an important part of their agenda. Sometimes a kiss is just a routine meeting of the lips, often in a perfunctory manner as a goodbye gesture or a "Hi, I'm home" announcement.

Going back a step further on the continuum: They report that they don't have the long talks, the sharing of ideas and feelings, that were so important to them when they courted. And, come to think of it, they don't really have dates anymore—"after all, we're married."

We are now left with sex on one end of the continuum and chitchat on the other end. No wonder intimacy withers and struggles for its very existence.

This need not be.

In the remainder of this book we will take up the banner marked with hearts and flowers and lettering that proclaims boldly: MORE INTIMATE MARRIAGES FOR ALL.

In the four chapters that follow, we will discuss the four important dimensions of an intimate marriage: emotional, intellectual, physical, and spiritual.

We will discuss ways in which wives and husbands can each be part of a campaign to enhance their marriages in each of these dimensions.

---

[1] *The Adventist Home,* p. 102.
[2] *Ibid.,* p. 106.

CHAPTER 5

Emotional Intimacy

Sometimes people get uneasy when we talk about emotions. It calls to mind something difficult to understand, to identify or cope with. To tell a woman "You are so emotional—just like a woman!" is generally not a compliment. Nor does a man feel complimented to be told that he wears his emotions on his sleeve. Most men believe that they are more "male" if they show emotions very sparingly.

Yet emotional intimacy in marriage concerns how well a wife and husband feel connected, cared for, loved, listened to, accepted, and cherished. We have a need to share deeply with someone to whom we have entrusted our love and faithfulness. Marriage provides the best setting for the growth of emotional intimacy, though it certainly does not guarantee it. Someone has facetiously said that developing an intimate relationship "comes about as naturally as learning the skill of brain surgery." Couples who find intimacy an elusive quality might agree.

When we consider three of the necessary ingredients for emotional intimacy, we can better understand how it can be difficult to realize. The first is a time commitment, the second is relationship skills, and the third is self-disclosure. We will now look at each of these.

Time commitment. Obviously this is vital. In this

frenzied world, couples find it difficult to devote specified minutes and hours for just the two of them. Some couples tell us that they even have difficulty making time for physical intimacy.

Relationship skills. This second ingredient, also known as interpersonal skills, makes it possible for the relationship to go beyond adequate to harmonious and need-filling. Our culture has not put much value on teaching interpersonal skills at any level—as if they will come naturally for most people. Divorce statistics belie this notion.

How we "get along" in our relationships affects our total existence. Our training for these skills is largely "on-the-job." Much of it is by trial and error: When behavior brings pain, we try to avoid that behavior. When avoidance seems to work, we mentally label it "this works." But if it doesn't work the next time, we get confused—and try something else.

Such mismanagement of relationships can cost us emotional stress, pain, and alienation. The more intimate the relationship is, the greater will be the cost. Since the marital relationship is surely the closest human relationship we enter into, it will feel its fair share of distress.

Perhaps this accounts for the great amount of interest Ellen White took in marriage and family matters. As people sought advice for their relationships, she spent great amounts of time writing out counsel suited to their individual needs. We have been blessed with two separate volumes of this counsel—preserved because it can be applicable to the needs of others. But we must never forget that the counsel was meant for specific people with specific problems, and though adaptable, it should not be applied to everyone across the board.

The Adventist Home and *Child Guidance* contain this material. Interestingly, at the time these books were compiled you couldn't find many books on Christian marriage and effective child-rearing techniques. Such topics were not on the tips of most tongues, as they are now. In fact, marriage was then considered more of a legal union than an emotional tie. Sharing feelings, values, and goals would seem foreign to wives addressing husbands formally as "Mr. Jones."

This is why it seems so remarkable that Ellen White wrote with such sensitivity and addressed so many emotionally involved issues. Marital interaction receives her pen's attention with great regularity. We will list here some of the themes that recur repeatedly in her books. They provide excellent guidelines for wives and husbands truly eager to have a relationship that is satisfying and growth-producing.

A brief suggestion: We are sometimes prone to read them as though they were written for our spouse only: "I surely hope Jeff pays attention to that third point" or "That is Emmy all over again." Instead, silently and thoughtfully read the list in a very self-confrontative manner: "Do I ever do that? . . . H'mm—I could really benefit by thinking that one through . . . As much as I hate to admit it, my behavior yesterday afternoon really ignored that counsel . . . Oops! This one's for me!"

With that caution in mind, look at the relationship skills Ellen White recommends.

1. Be quick to recognize the good qualities of the other.

2. Give love rather than exact it.

3. Express appreciation often.

4. Be gentle in speech.

5. Keep sharpness out of the voice.

6. Practice little courtesies.

7. Watch for chances to express affection and tender regard.

8. Don't make a practice of trying to get the other to follow your wishes.

9. Make a habit of encouraging each other.

All of these recommendations are taken from Sections V and VI of *The Adventist Home*. It is not by oversight that I have not included the page numbers where they are located. You will benefit by looking for them in these pages, since you will then find many other related suggestions.

Even a cursory look at this skills list reminds us how often communication is involved. This is not surprising, for it is the means by which we are known to one another. I do not plan to go deeply into that topic. There are many fine books on the market now to address this issue.

But I will mention that Scripture does a remarkable work of getting much valuable counsel into a small space. Attention to these exhortations alone would rescue many marriages from unnecessary pain, misunderstanding, argument, and alienation—

as well as solve the divorce problem. See if you don't agree.

Warnings

"A harsh word stirs up anger" (Prov. 15:1, NIV).

Temper is folly (Prov. 14:29).

Don't let unwholesome talk come out of your mouth (Eph. 4:29).

"Live at peace with everyone" (Rom. 12:18, NIV).

"Let us stop passing judgment on one another" (Rom. 14:13, NIV).

Love doesn't boast, isn't rude (1 Cor. 13:4, 5).

Love does not keep a record of wrongs (1 Cor. 13:5).

Promises

"A gentle answer turns away wrath" (Prov. 15:1, NIV).

He who guards his tongue keeps himself from calamity (James 3:2).

A patient man has understanding (Prov. 14:29).

"He who holds his tongue is wise" (Prov. 10:19, NIV).

Speaking the truth in love, we will in all things grow up into Him who is the head, Christ (Eph. 4:15).

And there are others—why not add them to this list as you find them?

Self-disclosure. While it is absolutely essential to intimacy, self-disclosure does not always elicit positive images. Our popular culture has made "telling all" almost a spectator sport—certainly it is a means of attracting publicity and making money. We decry the talk shows, radio call-ins, and endless printed exposés of verbal exhibitionists who reveal personal information for which there seems to be an insatiable audience. Christians will surely avoid being part of the market for this type of self-disclosure. When sharing parts of our lives with others becomes self-serving, it is suspect. When its purpose is to elicit sympathy or shock, when employed with any manipulative intent, it has missed the purposes we are proposing for consideration here.

Some feel that even when Christians talk to others about feelings connected with their problems, they are exhibiting weakness. The "stiff upper lip" school believes everyone should bravely keep such things to themselves. We occasionally will hear people lauded for "never once complaining," even through recurring violence or abuse. This type of silence is no virtue, and it often prevents both perpetrator and victim from receiving the help they need.

We find some very positive examples of self-disclosure in Scripture. Our heavenly Father has often shared His emotions. How much this has meant to us! How generously He has expressed His devoted care and endless acceptance. He tells us that He rejoices over us, He expresses confidence in us, and He lets us know how eager He is to be with us eternally. He shares with us His great heart of love, His pity, and His comfort as He is touched with our sadness. How impoverished our picture of God would be if these disclosures were not recorded. Hear our Elder

Brother say, "I have called you friends, for everything that I learned from my Father I have made known to you" (John 15:15, NIV). How we treasure His plans for us—right down to the rooms He now is preparing for us. In especially touching moments we are deeply affected when He shares with us His anguish and pain. We feel even closer to Him in our own pain, because we realize that He has been there before us.

Paul was also a "discloser." Not only did he teach, preach, and exhort; he shared personal experiences and feelings with his coworkers and converts. He offered explanations for his actions so that they might understand him better. He writes, "We loved you so much that we were delighted to share with you *not only the gospel of God but our lives as well, because you had become so dear to us*" (1 Thess. 2:8, NIV). In our interaction with others it is not enough to talk about the "head things"; the "heart things" are also part of our ministry.

Yet let's not overlook what preceded self-disclosure in Paul's account. Feelings of love and concern for the listener should precede sharing ourselves with others. These emotions give some protection against using disclosure solely for our own benefit (our own therapy), rather than the other's. Paul states that the purpose of his disclosures was for "building you up, not for tearing you down" (2 Cor. 13:10, NIV). Let's look at the important implications of that wise statement.

A "building-up" disclosure would encourage, support, and motivate. It would help one to realize that others had come through similar problems and can truly empathize. It might share steps another has taken to surmount them. The discloser could share how God had provided the courage needed on a day-by-day basis.

In contrast, the "tearing-down" type of disclosure would make the listener feel more distressed, insecure, and confused. It could give the already-burdened person an additional load. It would decidedly not be the atmosphere for emotional intimacy.

When you think about it, expressing love for our partner is self-disclosure. It is disclosing our feelings in a way that brings happiness and satisfaction. I have heard some spouses say that it shouldn't always be necessary to repeat our love and devotion, to express appreciation over and over again.

I don't know what incident prompted these words of Ellen White to her son Edson and his wife, but I treasure them: "No one in the world ever longed more earnestly for appreciation and fellowship than did Christ. He hungered for sympathy. His heart was filled with a longing desire that human beings might appreciate the gift of God to the world."[1]

And here's another thought. We are moved at how frequently God shares His love with us in Scripture. He finds many ways to let us know how dearly we are cherished, and how much we are valued in His loving thought. Rather than just saying it once—say, in John 3:16—God tells us of His great love again and again. Why is that? To be sure that we will never forget it? Yes, but I think there is a another deeper reason that really warms my heart.

He just *loves* to say it. This emotion is so strong that to utter it gives Him pleasure! I can understand that, can't you? Do you remember the first time you let the words fall from your lips? It is usually so memorable for most couples that they can tell you exactly where they were when they first spoke those words. That was a disclosure so wonderful!

Intimacy is nourished on words of love, appreciation, and sympathy. In intimate marriages, there will be no hesitancy in generously offering this love-preserver. Like their heavenly Father, His earthly sons and daughters—and husbands and wives—will often and eagerly express their love.

It is understandably more difficult for some spouses to share feelings. Not all of us were reared in homes in which parents talked to each other in loving tones and shared information and experiences that demonstrated their devotion to one another. Many of us may have "learned" that it was easier to stay out of trouble if we *didn't* talk about things such as frustration, resentment, or anger. Through the years we may have been frightened or reluctant to risk being laughed at, teased, or lectured. Expressing feelings, particularly negative ones, might have elicited responses such as "That was really dumb!"; "Why did you do that?"; "That's a silly way to feel"; or "Christians don't talk like that!"

Homes are not the only places that discourage telling about ourselves. Sometimes it can be an insensitive member of the extended family, a thoughtless neighbor, a teacher, or even a church member

who might give responses that show a lack of understanding. People will sometimes report, "I learned
early that the safest way to get along was just to keep
my mouth shut!"

Many husbands and wives, reporting on early experiences right after marriage when they felt more free
about self-disclosing, say they learned that it wasn't
such a good idea. Here are a few examples of responses that demonstrate why they are reluctant now:

- "You sound just like your mother."
- "You think you had a bad day—wait till you
  hear what happened to me."
- "You handled that wrong—this is what you
  should do."
- "I didn't mean anything by that—can't you
  take a joke?"

Tired of being ignored, interrupted, corrected,
and criticized, spouses refrain from opening themselves to each other—and in turn, cut themselves
off from the comfort, validation, encouragement, and
companionship that intimate marriages were designed by God to provide.

Spouses do not deliberately set about to sabotage
intimacy in their marriages. Most brides and grooms
plan for happiness, and indeed long for the intimacies
that they believe will come naturally with marriage.
Many are unaware that their words and actions can
prompt withdrawal and antagonism. When not reared
in a home that placed a premium on good communication, they have not come from a good "learning
place." If most of what is heard and observed is un-

worthy of imitation, a lot of repair work may need to be done to introduce more winsome ways of "wifing" and "husbanding."

I am stressing this because probably some of you are parents. You should realize that you are now providing your children with marital patterns that they will be prone to follow in future years. It is sobering to remember that we can affect the quality of our children's marriages.

We have talked about the responses that "choke off" self-disclosure. Here are some responses that make one glad they shared their feelings, values, and goals—so much so that they will do it regularly and eagerly:

- "Thank you for sharing that with me."
- "H'mm. That's an interesting viewpoint—it's a new thought to me."
- "It really makes me feel special when you confide in me."
- "I'm glad you told me how you feel about that—it makes me feel closer to you."
- "I can tell that really means a lot to you."
- "I really value your opinion."
- "I'm not sure I agree with that idea, but I appreciate your sharing it. Let me think about it." (And then do just that.)
- "When we share our ideas and thoughts like this, it makes me realize what emotional intimacy means; it's really a special 'married' feeling."
- "I used to dream about being able to talk things over like this—it is so great that we are getting better and better at it."

These are only suggestions, and obviously you will want to put them into your own words. Keep trying, and soon your responses will come naturally.

There are several very important general guidelines for sharing:

1. Listen! Don't let your mind wander or try to rehearse what you are going to say while your partner is talking. Pauses are good for conversations. They keep the head in gear and prevent runaway talking, which so often gets one into trouble. Keep your mind on what is being said. Look at your partner—and touch, if that will help keep you in the moment. One of the most precious gifts we can give our partner is undivided listening. It is a way of saying, "At this moment nothing is more important than what you are telling me, and I give my attention to you." (Why not try this right away?)

Find out what your current level of "listen-ability" is by answering the following questions. You probably will get some clues about how well you and your spouse are communicating. It will work with neighbors and bosses, too.

Check Your "Listen-ability"

1. Do you find it difficult to keep your mind from wandering when your mate is speaking?

2. When your mate is talking, do you try to sense how she/he is feeling about the matter being discussed?

3. Do certain phrases used by your mate prejudice you so that you cannot listen objectively (e.g., "my mother says . . ."; "the pastor thinks . . ."; etc.)?

4. When you are puzzled or annoyed by something that's been said, do you try to get the question straightened out before going on?

5. When you feel your mate is going on with greater detail and taking more time than you think is necessary, do you tune her/him out by reading, watching TV, or simply withdrawing?

6. When you don't feel like talking, do you pretend to pay attention as though you are listening but actually withdraw from the conversation?

7. Does your body language (eye contact, nodding, facial expressions) tell your mate that you are listening to what is being said?

8. Can you listen without being defensive in your mind when you disagree?

9. Are you an interrupter, eager to make your views known?

10. Do you ask your spouse to repeat ideas that are confusing or troubling?

11. Do you find yourself getting your next response ready while your mate is talking?

12. Can you respond with empathetic feedback even when you disagree?

13. Can you discuss your own and your spouse's answers to the above questions without denying, criticizing, blaming, or withdrawing?

2. Agreement is not the issue. You are entitled to your own thoughts, ideas, and opinions. Whether you are right or wrong isn't important. What is important is showing respect, love, and acceptance—prime ingredients of any kind of intimacy. Can couples share their disagreements? Of course! Sometimes it can be very stimulating to discuss these. But that may be "postgraduate" marriage communication! If you are finding that disagreements cause hurtful arguments, you are probably still at the "undergraduate level" of communication and will need some remedial work before you are ready to discuss issues that are dividing you.

3. Keep it clear. You each have a responsibility to clarify what you do not understand. If you don't understand a word, phrase, or sentence, ask for some help. Maybe the tone of voice doesn't seem to match what was being said—for instance, a loud, harsh voice talking about caring and cherishing. Express your confusion and ask for help in understanding the message you are getting.

4. Reward! Reward! Tell yourself how well you listened, how it really helped to touch, use eye contact, or talk winsomely. Then tell your spouse what was really meaningful for you about her/his listening behavior. Note any and all improvements. Remember, don't wait for perfection to compliment—improvement will do fine. Any small step in the right direction is cause for big-time celebration. You might even ask for feedback about your own responses. Hugs and kisses are good rewards too!

By now someone may be wondering whether it wouldn't be better just to avoid altogether communication that is not sunny, pleasant, and positive. Why not just repress all negative feelings? If we removed from Scripture anything but sunny, pleasant, positive communication, we wouldn't have much left. Out goes David, Solomon, and Elijah. Goodbye to Peter and Paul. We are not yet in that "land that is fairer than day," so for a while longer we will have to reckon with negative, hurtful, painful circumstances.

There are also some very good reasons that negative feelings must be shared. Unexpressed and consistently repressed feelings of anger and fear can cause emotional/psychological problems that can eventually explode in rage and violence. Unexpressed feelings can distance partners, damaging feelings of intimacy. On the other hand, if these feelings are shared with the purpose of removing barriers and bringing a better understanding, intimacy and trust will be enhanced. As Paul says, "Do not let any unwholesome talk come out of your mouths, but only what is helpful for building others up according to their needs, that it may benefit those who listen" (Eph. 4:29, NIV).

Health educators tell us that when people can confide their problems and concerns, their immune systems function better. This is another amazing example of how closely the systems of our body are interrelated. And no doubt one of the reasons we are exhorted to:

- 〜 Share one another's burdens! (see Gal. 6:2).
- 〜 "Confess your sins to each other and pray for each other" (James 5:16, NIV).
- 〜 "Rejoice with those who rejoice; mourn with those who mourn" (Rom. 12:15, NIV).

❧ "Be kind and compassionate to one another" (Eph. 4:32, NIV).

❧ "Encourage one another and build each other up" (1 Thess. 5:11, NIV).

Conclusions

Emotional intimacy is not easy to attain, nor is it an invariable state. Couples feel more emotionally intimate at some times than others. Pause to talk together about the times you feel most intimate with each other. It would not be at all surprising if your partner had a different "intimacy gauge" than you do. Be glad that you know when you can add to your spouse's feelings of married intimacy—what a privilege! And it's yours alone.

Finally, realize that emotional intimacy needs continual attention and nurture. Ellen White once counseled, "The real union of the two in wedlock is the work of the afteryears."[2] She also made the interesting comment that "it would be more appropriate to let some of the hours of courtship before marriage run through the married life."[3] Isn't *that* a great observation!

But here is the capstone—the word of encouragement we all need as we seek to bring heaven into our marriages: "God is love and by His grace you *can succeed* in making each other happy, as in your marriage vows you promised to do."[4]

In this chapter we have emphasized the importance of emotional intimacy through effective communication. Since there can be no intimacy without emotions, sharing feelings is crucial. Read through the following exercise with your spouse. Checking the appropriate box could help put into words what is sometimes difficult to share verbally. Remember, the true value of doing this together is the discussion that can follow.

Communicating for Intimacy

1. I don't share my inner feelings with my partner because
- ❏ she/he is not interested.
- ❏ I don't want to bother her/him with them.
- ❏ I have never been able to express myself very well.
- ❏ she/he doesn't share feelings either; it's a pattern.
- ❏ even though I would like to, it seems to threaten my partner.

2. It's hard for me to discuss my weaknesses and failures because
- ❏ my partner might think less of me.
- ❏ my partner would say I'm exaggerating.
- ❏ my partner might say I'm silly to feel that way.
- ❏ she/he might not listen, and then I'd really feel bad.

3. If I did share, I wish my partner would
- ❏ hug me, comfort me, and tell me I'm great!
- ❏ tell me what I'm doing wrong and correct me.
- ❏ give me advice on how I could handle things.

❑ try to make jokes and tease me out of my feelings.

4. It's hard for us to talk over our problems together because
   ❑ we get into arguments and end up angry or hurting.
   ❑ we usually skip them and hope for the best.
   ❑ we usually end up doing what my partner suggests.
   ❑ we don't have a dependable method for problem-solving.
5. When my partner hurts my feelings
   ❑ I let it go. She/he will be defensive if I bring it up, and I'll end up feeling misunderstood.
   ❑ I wonder what I've done wrong now!
   ❑ I tell my partner, and she/he says I'm too sensitive.
   ❑ I tell my partner, we talk it over, accept apologies, and make up (sometimes with loving enthusiasm!).

6. If we should have problems in the area of sexuality
   ❑ we never have problems.
   ❑ we never discuss it—it's too embarrassing.
   ❑ we would share what we are experiencing comfortably.
   ❑ we would seek help through reading or counseling.
   ❑ I could count on my spouse to be sensitive and loving.
   ❑ I would feel comfortable talking to my spouse

about what I think would enhance our sexuality for me.

[1] *This Day With God,* p. 189.
[2] *The Adventist Home,* p. 105.
[3] *Ibid.,* p. 56.
[4] *Ibid.,* p. 112.

CHAPTER 6

Intellectual Intimacy

Intellectual intimacy has to do with how people share ideas and viewpoints about the world around them. This could proceed from such activities as reading together—or separately and then reporting. It might include going to meetings or lectures together, and then spending time evaluating the ideas presented. Sometimes couples like to attend classes on shared interests—home improvement, nature, foreign language, current events, political issues, child-rearing. Most people are well aware that they will not be able to depend on the newspapers or television to sharpen their intellects.

Ellen White commented on the value of women reading so they could keep themselves companionable with their husbands and in touch with their children.[1] I believe we could give husbands the same admonition. However, when she was writing, women were not encouraged to know much about the world outside their homes, so she addressed her remarks to them.

In addition to the study possibilities noted above, couples should be alert for any offerings on enhancing marital relationships. Topics might include communication, conflict resolution, decision-making, role assignments, and preparing for retirement. Another intellectual pursuit is marriage enrichment meetings.

It is always interesting for a marriage therapist to hear couples tell the story of their romance. Very often one or the other—or both—will report nostalgically about the way they were able to talk about so many things together. "We would spend hours in each other's company, just talking." About what? They can scarcely remember. They just recall the pleasure they had talking about "all kinds of things." Few couples realize how truly important is the time spent in conversation with each other.

Sometimes you can gauge the health of a marriage by finding out how much time couples do talk casually each day. One young woman admitted that talking was one of the main reasons she chose her husband. "We talked together so well!" she says, adding that the habit has continued. "When we get done in the kitchen after supper and the children are in bed, we often sit out on the porch swing and just talk about everything that happened during the day: something we read or heard on the radio, news from our friends and families, the weather, the phase of the moon, our plans for next year's vacation—and yes, some dreams and some memories, too! And when we are doing this, I think, *This is about as good as life can get!*"

"That sounds great," someone is saying. "But my spouse won't talk like that. He/she is the quiet, silent type."

Everyone *does* talk some. But there may be reasons it isn't happening for you as it is for the young couple above. When people don't come from "talking families," they may find it hard to make casual conversation. Others may find "small talk" difficult because they like to think over carefully what they want to say—after all, they might be called to account for a word or phrase if they misspeak. Some may use silence as a way of controlling or staying distant, which means that both their partner and they are missing the intellectual intimacy that talking can provide.

It is also possible that the difference in the way that women and men communicate can be a roadblock. Women generally are more interested in details, and this often tires men who want to get to the point. Women view conversations with their husbands as a time of closeness—they like it to last. Never mind if content is not earthshaking, it fills a need for being together in a way that a TV sitcom never can—unless you give equal time after you turn it off to discuss it! Spending time talking together gives importance to the relationship. It says, "I value our relationship and want to nurture it by talking/visiting/chatting together."

When we decide to begin a new behavior pattern, we need to start with realistic expectations. You probably won't be the couple on the porch swing by tomorrow. Begin slowly and deliberately by setting aside just five minutes—maybe 10. Avoid things you know you disagree on. But do have at least a tiny agenda. Sitting down and saying, "Well, what do you want to talk about?" may not work.

Your tiny agenda might include any of the following: the best thing that has happened so far today, what's on your "must do" list this week, something funny or amazing you heard or read today, your pride in the accomplishment of someone close to you, how you might help a friend with a weighty problem, etc. You will be surprised how soon you will be chatting away together—without notes—and loving it.

Another important value of intellectual intimacy is its protectiveness. For example, if you're feeling stressed or alienated from your spouse, you might be attracted to someone who may seem "more understanding." At this time you need a strong dose of intellectual processing. Your mind will tell you why fidelity is a better choice than what your emotions are recommending.

In counseling one couple with this problem, Ellen White said, "It should henceforth be the life study of both husband and wife how to avoid everything that creates contention and to keep unbroken the marriage vows." [2] Isn't that a class A statement! It covers two issues—avoiding contention and keeping marriage vows.

Christians generally agree that keeping marriage vows is of utmost importance, and church boards and pastors often try to solve the problems that always fall in the wake of those who choose not to honor their vows. Church leaders spend many committee hours studying ways to promote fidelity and strong moral values in marriage relationships, as well as seeking to frame policies for situations in which marital vows are broken. That is necessary.

But I wonder why we have not paid more attention to the first part of that statement—that couples should make a life study (an intellectual exercise) of how to avoid "everything that causes contention." If we would work harder on that part of the counsel, keeping our marriage vows would be "as easy as falling off a log."

Aren't you glad Ellen White mentions that both husband and wife should be involved in this study process? Many times people feel that the quality of the marriage relationship falls more heavily on the wife (which was particularly true when Ellen White wrote this). But that would cheat the marriage.

In my years as a marriage therapist, I have never yet talked to a couple who could not tell me what their problem (contention) consisted of—and usually each had a pretty clear idea of whose problem it was . . .

"Sandy just can't stay on a budget—she spends too much money."

"Bill won't take any responsibility around the house or with the children, and we both work full-time. It's not fair!"

"Jan is always calling her mother, and she tells her everything that goes on here." "Every difference of opinion we have mushrooms into a big argument with yelling and name-calling. We just can't talk things over."

"Jim is so thoughtless. He doesn't think to let me know when he is going to be home late."

"My mother kept things looking decent, and I could count on having clean socks and underwear in my drawer."

"We can't agree on how to discipline our children. Our ideas are worlds apart."

"We have different ideas on how to spend our Sabbaths. Ellie came from a very legalistic family, and she thinks everything but singing and praying is wrong."

"Jeff isn't nearly as demonstrative and loving as he was before we were married. He thinks sex is the answer to everything—well, it's not for me!"

"Mary Ann plans all my time. She has appointed herself our social secretary, and tells me what we are going to do and who we are going to be with. I had some good friends before we were married, and I'd like to play handball and ride bikes occasionally. Forget that! She pouts and says I don't love her anymore. She acts as though I'm deserting her. I'd like a little input into the management of my time."

You might be interested to know that the above dismal recital of problems are among those most frequently presented in therapy. They concern the handling of money (always rates high), the rearing of children, communication problems, clashes over in-laws, role assignments, quarrels over sexuality, and disagreements about religious values. If you have problems in these areas, you are not alone.

Since these contentious issues may change through the life stages of a marriage, Ellen White wisely says that it should be a *life* study. It is cheering to know that there are more resources for this type of study than ever before. Books and helps, many of them with self-teaching exercises, can be found in many bookstores and libraries. Getting acquainted with your local library is definitely in the "intellectual intimacy" category. Communication seminars are often available through community organizations, schools, and churches. The Family Services Department of the General Conference of Seventh-day Adventists has created some outstanding materials to be used by local church groups. These are constructed so that they do not require a college professor or a psychologist to conduct them (though some of these persons have been involved in putting them together). They are professional quality.

If your church has not been involved in "life study" activities, talk to your pastor and find out if your church nominating committee has appointed a family life leader for your congregation. Perhaps that person, or someone they might suggest, could lead out in programs for engaged couples, married couples, parents, and single parents who often feel they have additional problems. The above-mentioned materials are so well constructed that even those leaders without much experience could feel comfortable.

Professional Counseling

There may come a time when marital contention is so intense that professional counseling will be necessary. Even this is a "learning" experience, with the counselor as the "teacher" helping the clients explore the troubling situation, not only emotionally but intellectually.

Some people feel that unless they can consult a Christian counselor, they are at risk. Good counselors and therapists are trained not to work against the moral values of their clients. They have no intent to propose interventions that will bring more confusion into the picture than already exists. They have a vested interest in helping, not harming.

It is true that occasionally we hear of situations in which the language or content of a session has bordered on the objectionable. One of the purposes of a counseling relationship is learning to share what you are thinking and feeling. If you feel uncomfortable with a therapist's style or content, let him/her know. This will demonstrate that you are good client material, since you have the ego strength to speak up for yourself. Nor is it improper as you begin your first session to mention to your therapist that you are a conservative Christian, and that you are interested in working with someone who will honor that value. It is possible that you may have to look for another counselor, but before you change make sure *your own reluctance* to work on your problems is not intervening and causing difficulty in the counseling sessions.

There are many fine counselors who can be contacted through referral from your pastor, community resource centers, or the yellow pages. Some will identify themselves as Christian counselors. Occasionally the local Council of Churches knows which denominations have counseling centers. Make sure that your therapist is properly credentialed in your state—they are obligated to display their licenses and other credentials in their offices. I firmly believe that God expects us to do everything we can to preserve the marriages to which we have vowed continuing faithfulness.

Positive Intellectual Intimacy

In the preceding chapter on emotional intimacy, we looked at positive ways to respond to your partner's sharing of feelings and sentiments. Here are some positive ways to respond to your partner's sharing of ideas and viewpoints:

- "I hadn't thought of it that way—tell me more about that."
- "A lot of people might agree with you."
- "I'd have to think about that some more."
- "It sounds like you really feel strongly about that."
- "I think it is interesting that we feel so similar (or differently) about that."
- "I've heard that the longer people live together, the more they think alike."
- "I wonder if that will happen to us."
- "I can understand why they say that healthy couples talk together a lot. I feel we're healthier already!"
- "I really appreciate your taking this time for us to talk. It makes me feel cherished (or important, or worthwhile, or whatever)."
- "I'm not good at expressing myself. Thanks for your patience."

You will note that the statements above don't argue, contradict, or deny the other person his/her viewpoint. Most important, they express positive sentiments and appreciation for the other person's input. That is crucial if sharing is to become a treasured part of your intimacies. *Remember: There is no intimacy without sharing.*

Expressing Love

Dick looked at Terry in disbelief. "How can you seriously say that you aren't sure I love you? I know I'm not good at the ways your parents show love—hugging and kissing and calling each other pet names. My family just didn't go in for stuff like that. In fact, they thought that some of those demonstrations were, well, sort of inappropriate. Look, I pay the bills, wash the cars every Friday, and you know I have never been unfaithful to you. Isn't that love?"

Then there was Sue, who tried to convince Josh that her actions are full of demonstrations of her love. "Josh, I keep the house the way you like it—I keep the vases full of flowers from the garden, and on Friday afternoon I try to have the smell of chocolate brownies permeating the air when you come home. You know I am careful with our household expenses. I do these things because I love you. Why do I have to keep verbalizing it all the time?"

There are many ways of expressing love and, obviously, both Dick and Sue are successful at some of these ways. And that's good! So why are their spouses not satisfied? Each person has her/his own way of defining loving behavior. Love means most when it follows a person's mental images of a loving marriage. These images come from what they saw in their own homes, what they absorb from their reading, and what they observe in others. It is important to manifest love to our spouses in ways that are meaningful to them, as well as in ways that we feel are significant.

The following list is composed of expressions of

love that wives and husbands report are most important to them. Check the ones that are special to you, and it will help your partner know what to emphasize in demonstrating love. As you talk them over, tell why you think these expressions have become favorites for you.

Love Can Be Expressed in Many Ways

Express love by:

- ❑ saying "I love you."
- ❑ using special "pet" names that have meaning.
- ❑ voicing expressions of affirmation and approval, such as "You look great" and "I love being with you."
- ❑ being aware of facial expressions, tones, gestures.
- ❑ expressing total commitment, permanence, loyalty.
- ❑ touching affectionately, patting, caressing, stroking, cuddling, etc.
- ❑ showing appreciation and gratitude.
- ❑ complimenting about ability, values, etc.
- ❑ remembering special occasions—anniversaries, birthdays, Valentine's Day, etc.
- ❑ positive things about you to others.
- ❑ looking for things to do together.
- ❑ disclosing my feelings, ideas, thoughts, dreams, goals, disappointments to you.
- ❑ giving emotional support, comforting, empathizing.
- ❑ tolerating frustrations without blowing up (having a "long fuse").

❑ buying, or making, gifts.

❑ notes that express affection and caring.

❑ listening with interest when I talk to you.

❑ attending to personal hygiene and dress.

❑ helping you with jobs or chores.

❑ planning surprises—phone calls, poems, notes, etc.

❑ being emotionally and sexually faithful.

❑ being willing to continue to work on our relationship.

❑ negotiating disagreements—being willing to give and take.

❑ laughing and having fun with you.

❑ sharing a devotional time with you.

Whenever I read the following sentence in *The Adventist Home,* I have delightful mind pictures of husbands and wives sitting together in their family rooms, living rooms, patios, wherever, enjoying time together listening to one another and sharing. Here it is: "Jesus wants to see happy marriages, happy firesides." [3]

What picture does your mind paint?

---

[1] *The Adventist Home,* p. 23.

[2] *Ibid.,* p. 85.

[3] *Ibid.,* p. 99.

CHAPTER 7

Sexual Intimacy

Sometimes near the beginning of a seminar on intimacy someone will ask, "When are you going to talk about *real* intimacy?" For many, it is difficult to think of intimacy in anything but physical terms.

But how are couples to know the full extent of sexuality in their lives? There has never been much eagerness in homes, schools, and churches to talk forthrightly about sexuality. Pause and recall where you received most of your information about this vital part of your personhood. This will be very important in helping you to understand each other's attitudes and even how each responds in sexual situations.

I hope your sexual information came from your parents—each talking with you about your concerns and giving you important information, on schedule, about the physical changes you would experience in puberty and adolescence. Then, hopefully, you discussed what sexuality involves at each life stage.

"No," you say, "it didn't happen that way for me." That is not surprising—it doesn't happen that way for many. Someone may think that my scenario for home-centered sexual education may be too idealistic. But I make no apologies for that. To tell you the truth, I am longing for the ideal, and the closer we can come to this ideal, the better. Parents must begin early and educate factually and sensitively for sexuality if we are to bring about happier marriage relationships.

When there is no such communication about sexuality as they grow up, children have no vocabulary to make discussion possible. So to avoid embarrassment, parents, teachers, and church leaders simply ignore comprehensive discussions and settle for prohibitions and warnings. As a result, most sexual information comes from the media, and that message will be loud and clear: "Sex is to enjoy, everybody is doing it, get yours!" Since this message is incompatible with Christian values, confusion ensues. The outcome?

1. Sexuality is not seen in its true beauty.

2. Sexuality is often relegated to a lower value, a "regrettable necessity."

3. God is seen as disapproving of our natural impulses rather than being their creator.

4. God's guidelines are seen as arbitrary restrictions rather than loving protection from heartache, disorganization, and illness.

5. The average Christian has a hard time integrating sexuality into his/her faith.

6. Since our Lord Himself was celibate, we are not sure He understands our feelings, our desires, our expectations, and our problems.

7. Sometimes it seems as though our church has a hard time approving of the celebration of sexuality, while at the same time respecting its limits.

Let's think through some of the things we know about human equality. God created us male and female, with the capability to unite bodies in the sexual embrace. God gave this special gift to humans not only for the purpose of populating the earth, but also to be a unifying and pleasurable experience between wives and husbands. Some people have difficulty understanding this twofold emphasis. But let us remember that the Creator could have planned for pregnancy to be the result of a purely biological incident. Husbands and wives could have been made aware of the procedure to follow when they wished to have children, and carried through the plan in a completely emotionless manner, unattended by sexual desire and pleasure.

The earth could have been successfully populated via a purely mechanical procedure. Pleasure is not necessary for impregnation. Furthermore, when women come to the time in life when conception is no longer possible, it would have been reasonable for the pleasure component to cease. But as God planned it, long past the age of childbearing, both women and men continue to enjoy sexual pleasure and orgasms, many times to a greater degree (since she feels that she has more freedom for sexual activity when the possibility of pregnancy is removed). We can feel confident that it was part of God's overall plan for women and men to have the capacity and desire for bonding in a one-flesh experience.

The act of this meeting of bodies has been described in the Bible in very descriptive words. Solomon in Proverbs 5:19 wishes that a man will always be "captivated" (NIV) by his wife's love. This word has also been translated as ravished, delighted, transported, intoxicated, and transcended. It becomes very clear that we are not considering here a ho-hum experience! Someone has termed orgasm in lovemaking as an "extravagance of nature." Don't fail to note the words of ecstasy and joyousness provided for us in the inspired words of the Song of Solomon, which are expressed by both the female and male lovers. It is interesting to note in this connection that neither of the lovers in the Song of Solomon mention any expectation of their love being a necessary forerunner of parenting, which was at that time a highly coveted expectation. Again and again we are helped in understanding that God meant married sexuality to be no average gift—but then His gifts never are.

Sexuality in Eden

At this point we will consider the circumstances when Adam and Eve first experienced their one-fleshness after Creation in order to make our own setting as close to theirs as we can.

1. There was great beauty. Everything that God had created for their pleasure was brand-new and untouched by the blight of sin. It is difficult for us to picture such perfection of flower and tree, shrub and plant. Each of their senses was appealed to as they looked about them. The Edenic marital bed was not marred by disorder. It was not necessary to throw the books and magazines in the corner to be able to turn the bed down. There was no collection of unfolded clothes just out of the dryer to cope with. (But if there had been, I think Adam would have helped Eve fold them and put them away.) As comanagers of their environment, Adam and Even were to be partners in subduing it (Gen. 1:28, NIV), and that certainly would include enhancing their living space.

You say it's not fair to compare Eden with your bedroom? You are right, of course. They had many advantages. But I believe that it is still appropriate to suggest a "look around" together at the location of your love trysts. There may be some minor changes that can make it more special for both of you. You might decide to add framed prints of fields of flowers, a waterfall, a pastoral scene, or whatever type of natural beauty that stirs your senses. Then add a basket of silk flowers tastefully arranged, an angel figurine, a framed wedding photo of the two of you, some incense and a bottle of cologne to spray the sheets, and most certainly a candleholder and candles on the nightstand with a packet of matches in the top drawer. Have fun thinking it over and bring some beauty into your setting in the next few weeks.

2. There was complete privacy. "Oh, sure—that was easy there!" someone demurs. But it is very important to feel your private marital space consists of just the two of you, your marriage bed, and your love. Even after children arrive, you can make (creative) plans to be uninterrupted for this love time.

But there is yet another privacy that the first pair enjoyed—mental privacy. Their minds had complete "privacy" from *anything* that belittled, trivialized, or degraded sexuality. They had never heard a dirty joke. No one had given them the impression that sexuality was coarse, vulgar, undignified, shameful, or embarrassing. Weren't they fortunate? They didn't have to surmount impressions of sexuality that might affect their attitudes and therefore their enjoyment.

Think of it then: a woman and a man with two perfect bodies having every nerve and muscle in a state of perfection, two minds filled only with love for each other, and the wonder of what femaleness and maleness meant in their lives. What an awesome event their first sexual experience must have been! Remind yourselves—this is just what God desires for all married couples.

3. There was interpersonal harmony. Not until sin entered the garden do we have a record of a rift in the relationship between Eve and Adam. Blame and relinquishing of personal responsibility surfaced— both incompatible with intimacy. Studies indicate that when women feel good about their interpersonal relationship with their husbands, they enjoy their sexual experiences more and therefore are more eager to be partners. In fact, it is one of the first qualities mentioned as being important to them in their sexual enjoyment. Apparently, when a good interpersonal relationship is alive and well, she will judge sex as more pleasing.

4. There was equality. Adam and Eve were absolute equals. Ellen White tells us plainly they were created as equals.[1] There is no doubt about God's ideal for their status. Actually He took unusual care to make sure that they understood His plan. Let's look at the interesting sequence of Creation. God created

Adam first and let him experience being without a suitable companion for a time, perhaps just long enough to realize his lonely state. You recall God having made the observation "It is not good for the man to be alone" (Gen. 2:18, NIV). Of course, this was no surprise to God. The creating Trio had these two in mind from the inception of creation planning. But the timing did help Adam to realize that his solitary situation was unique and unenviable.

So God gave Adam the surprise of his short life. Note again the manner in which He did it: God deliberately put Adam to sleep. God was about to do something absolutely astounding, yet He put Adam to sleep and deprived him of witnessing it. Why? True, He planned to use material from Adam's side in a beautiful bit of symbolism—Eve was to stand by his side as his equal, not in any other hierarchical relationship. But God, being God, could have accomplished this by the means of bloodless, painless surgery. He could simply have asked Adam to stand still, and then removed the body tissue.

Could it be that God didn't want Adam to feel that he had any part whatsoever in the creation of Eve? Adam might later say, "I was there. I watched God as you were created." Or even: "When we made you . . . " This would have put Adam in a "one-up" situation, and that would have been contrary to the equality that God intended.

Perhaps if we had more carefully considered the circumstances surrounding human creation, we would have been sufficiently motivated to work our way back to the Eden-ideal of equality, and could have avoided the pain, disorganization, and divisiveness that the "male superiority" mentality has caused. It would surely have diminished some of the sexual problems that multiply when the equality safeguard is ignored: polygamy, prostitution, rape, abuse, violence, molestation, and incest.

Even today when the quality of sexual interaction between married partners is studied, couples who feel they have a "marriage of equals" rate their entire marriage relationship, as well as their sexual loving, as much more satisfactory than do couples in which either spouse feels that their wife/husband is dominant.

5. There was sanctioned sexuality. From the beginning of their sexual relationship, Eve and Adam had no misguided concern about the seemliness of their physical intimacy. It was created and sanctioned by God. They knew that the feelings their bodies were experiencing were just what God had planned. God was not only the creator of these desires and yearnings; He was their instructor in explaining "one-fleshness" to them. It dishonors God to think He would leave Friday evening with only the brief comment "Be fruitful and multiply," since they knew absolutely nothing about being fruitful and multiplying. It is not like our God to leave us in ignorance and in confusion. I am convinced that He explained to them in its beautiful purity just exactly how they were to share in this intimacy. As a sexual educator of many years, I long to know just what words God used, how He gave them the good news about this part of their creation. I hope to ask Him someday!

Into the World . . .

With reluctance we move from the garden into the world, in which sexuality fared less well. Through the centuries many influences left their mark on the thinking about sexuality—dualism, asceticism, hedonism, evolution, Puritanism, and liberalism and modernism. All have added ideas still part of our present thinking. These philosophies have often taken from sexuality its beauty and removed it from its center, in God's love. "Love can no more exist without revealing itself in outward acts," wrote Ellen White, "than fire can be kept alive without fuel."[2]

We would not want to leave this discussion with the notion that the only aspect of sexual intimacy is genital/physical manifestation. There is an important area of intimacy that includes nongenital touching. These expressions are very important to the relationship, for both women and men, though women generally rank them as more important than men do. Pay attention, men: Demonstrations of love that do not have as their immediate goal sexual intercourse are extremely important to your wife. One common source of dissatisfaction for many women is that they do not get enough hugs, kisses, caresses, and loving touches during the day—the kind that do not lead directly to total intimacy.

I believe we have laid far too much emphasis on just intercourse and orgasm, and we need to realize the great contribution of nonintercourse touching and enjoyment. Ellen White refers to these expressions as "an affectionate attachment," "early attentions," "little attentions," "a tender interest," and "love's precious influence." There is a whole repertoire of "outward acts" that are very important to the growth and maintenance of your intimacy.

You have already discussed, in chapter 4, the importance of these actions as you moved on your own "love continuum" from hand-holding to marriage. Now let's name again some of the activities that married people enjoy: hand-holding, hugging, cuddling, nestling, patting, stroking, rubbing, tracing with the fingers on each other's bodies, caressing, affectionate words and deeds, leaving notes and/or cards for each other to find, gifts (whose value is not in the price tag but in the thought accompanying them—a red rose on the pillow may mean more than a new waffle iron), sincerely complimenting, expressing appreciation, sharing an anecdote or an experience from your day.

And now it's your turn. Talk about your favorite affectionate attentions. *Caution:* Do lots of listening. No criticism, judging, or withdrawing. Listen carefully and thoughtfully. We learn so much more from listening than we do from talking. Think about this comment of Stephen Covey's *Seven Habits of Highly Effective People:* "Most people do not listen with the intent to understand; they listen with the intent to reply."

Components of Sexuality

Now let's move on to three of the most important components of sexuality in marriage.

1. Commitment. Without the complete assurance that each member of the marriage partnership is totally committed "till death do us part," there can be no complete giving of oneself in the marriage embrace. One cannot risk the most personal and unique aspect of personhood if there is a concern that it could eventually be rejected, neglected, or replaced. Experiencing and partaking of each other's deepest wells of love can only be meaningful if it is restricted to one other—one's "God-united" beloved.

2. Total intimacy. Without a closeness that encompasses the emotional, the intellectual, and the spiritual, it cannot truly be called intimacy. When two lovers are within each other's life boundaries, they are sharing at a level unique to the marital relationship—a space that is closed to others. This ideal is not achieved during the honeymoon; it is a lifetime growth process. It should never be taken for granted, but made the focus of much of their time together.

3. Knowledge of the physical act of intimacy. Sometimes marrying couples are tempted to feel that, with the media constantly at hand, they know all about sexuality. But knowing the terminology is different from understanding all that is involved in the four phases of the sexual response pattern: excitement, love-play, orgasm, and resolution. (I will not here repeat the material covered in another book I have written, *Captivated by Love.*) Knowledge can help to release inhibitions and answer questions that are causing anxiety and dysfunction.

Right here would be a good place to report that the Seventh-day Adventist Church, in response to sexual problems present in church memberships around the world, called for a conference in October 1997. Representatives from each world division were called to attend the World Commission on Human Sexuality, in Washington, D.C. One of the outstanding conclusions was that the church must be involved in educating about Christian sexuality in our homes, schools, and churches. Materials with worldwide relevance and applicability are being prepared.

Rescuing the Sexual Experience

In the meantime, what can wives and husbands do to rescue, restore, or enhance their sexual experience?

1. Dispel the "naturalisim" myth. Sexual matters do not just naturally take care of themselves. Marriage partners will need to give time and effort not only to understanding what intimacy involves, but how to achieve it. They will need to understand what part their individual backgrounds might have in their responses to each other. They will need to talk—and listen.

2. Do not allow the messages of perversion and violence to color the whole area of sexuality. This is not easy, given the bombardments of the media. Even when young people in surveys tell us that most of what they know about sex comes through the media, complacency seems to prevent them from taking a firm stand against the innuendos and explicit materials contained in soap operas, situation comedies, videos, and movies. These portrayals can become such an addiction that the most elaborate rationalizations are given for watching them. Sexual love cannot continue to be a noble and tender emotion for young or old if it is incessantly bombarded by these inappropriate and immoral messages.

Sexuality can still be pure and beautiful in our minds. We can still see God's plan as a precious gift to our marriage, if we prayerfully invest our efforts in discriminating the bad and ugly from the beautiful.

3. Keep sexuality sacred. Though marriage often begins in a religious setting employing sacred themes, many couples are soon separated from spiritual influences, and God is not considered the basis or fount of their love. When couples forgo God's presence in their relationship, they are losing something very precious. (More on this in the next chapter.)

4. Enjoy life. Most couples need to learn all over again how to have fun together—how to laugh, share funny incidents, make jokes, and so on. Earnest Christians sometimes have difficulty with that. They seem concerned that, in this troubled world, we need to emphasize that "life is earnest, life is real." Frequently when dysfunctional couples seek marriage counseling, it has been quite some time since they have "rejoiced and been exceeding glad." Love has a difficult time thriving in this environment.

How do you increase your "fun"? Start by making a list of the things you used to enjoy when you were dating. Which activities were the most fun? When did you laugh the hardest?

By the way, have you ever checked a Bible concordance to see how many entries appear under the word "rejoice"? There are several pages of texts. "Rejoice" is a very hearty word. It means more than a weak smile. Solomon reminds us that there is a time to laugh. When is your time? Find out together!

You have probably heard of the medical benefits of laughter, which include reduction of stress, a positive outlook, even building up your immune system. Marriage has an "immune system" too. If you want to be immune from the blahs—from negative feelings about your relationship—indulge in a good laugh regularly. Then watch your pleasure in each other grow. Notice how you feel less critical, more accepting, more forgiving.

I should report on those couples who start their marriage therapy in a solemn, heavy state. They unwittingly demonstrate something very interesting. As the weeks go by, as they begin to see improvements in their relationship, they become more hopeful and begin to see each other through more understanding eyes. And they present a "lighter" feeling. They might even come in laughing over something funny that happened in the parking lot, or yesterday, or to report some lark they are planning for next weekend.

Try this Rejoice! formula for yourselves. Don't expect instant results. But if you persist, you will be rewarded with a new feeling of joyousness.

5. *Understand the problems that can interfere with sexual pleasure.* Here I am going to combine the

many women's voices and men's voices I have listened to. These three themes are often repeated.

Women say:

1. I wish my husband could understand that sex for me is more than a nighttime episode. I want to feel loved and cherished all day. It can begin with a tender hug and kiss when we part in the morning, perhaps a phone call during the day, a caress as he passes my chair while we are reading in the evening, with compliments and words of endearment interspersed throughout. I don't feel very loving when the first evidence I have of his caring starts with sexual touching after we're in bed. My husband has no idea how responsive I might be if he could be demonstrative outside of the bed!

2. Sometimes I have the feeling that physical expression for my husband is simply a need for sexual tension release. I have read that it generally takes women longer to become sexually aroused, and that certainly seems to be true for me. I don't like to get the feeling that I am "holding things up." I have these visions of us lying in each other's arms, taking the time to talk about our love, how lucky we are to have each other, what could we do to make our love more wonderful, and things like that. If lovemaking is so desirable, why hurry it up?

3. My husband seems to feel belittled or almost insulted if I mention to him something I wish he would do differently—or some way in which he could pleasure me. I know he was more sexually experienced

when we married, and I sort of expected him to be the "leader" in sexual matters. But now I realize that I am a part of this sexual event, and I would like to speak for myself—like the Shulammite maid did to Solomon—and have a part in suggesting some of our love repertoire. I have done some reading and know that my ideas are not inappropriate. When I mention that I would like this touch to be softer, or that caress to last longer, he seems to resent it. Sometimes he follows through, but only for that occasion, then he returns to his usual style of lovemaking. I say "lovemaking," but this attitude doesn't generate feelings of love in me.

Men say:

1. I wish my wife would be more involved in our sexual intimacies. I sort of expected that I would be the initiator—I guess that's the way it usually is. But I didn't expect my wife to be so, well, detached. I'd like to feel that I can be a sensitive and effective lover, but I don't know how to bring her into this experience. She just lies there and doesn't talk or move much. Sometimes when I ask her if there is anything I can do to pleasure her, she says something like "It's OK." I wish I could feel that our lovemaking was pleasurable for her, too.

2. I have read that men usually want to make love more often than women do, and I think I was prepared for that. But I didn't expect to feel like an ogre when I initiated sex. I think my wife was reared to believe that all men wanted of their wives was sex, and

this has affected her thinking. When I start to initiate loving her, she sighs and gives a "Not again" signal. Even when she acquiesces, it isn't with much enthusiasm. I can understand that there are times she would rather not make love, and I can go along with that. But I wish she could make it seem more like a loving postponement than an insensitive denial.

3. When we first brought our son home from the hospital, I was the happiest man alive. I had always looked forward to being a father—but I didn't realize that it came with a change in our sexual lives. My wife's desire took a long time to return, and even then it was always secondary to the baby's, the toddler's, and now our little boy's needs. I sometimes feel like a third-rate member of the family. I long for the feeling of being my wife's love mate again. Our son is the source of some of the greatest joy I have known, but I would like to feel that our love—my wife's and mine—is still the primary love relationship in the family. My wife is probably right—we should have another child to make our family complete. But I don't look forward to another sexual drought.

For different reasons, lovemaking is a higher priority for some people than for others. While it is part of what wives and husbands can expect from marriage when they marry, it should not be thought of as a "right" to be demanded. It is a privilege to be sought. A sexual relationship that is satisfying to both partners can make a good marriage even better. However, there are some happy, long-married couples who for various reasons would not evaluate their sexual experience as highly satisfactory. Couples rarely divorce if their relationship is excellent in every area but sexuality. Neither do they stay together if their sexual experience is the only good thing about their marriage. The ideal, of course, is for wives and husbands to take good care of all parts of their marital interaction.

I include these vignettes to help both wives and husbands know that their problems are not unique. The key ingredient toward a better understanding of each other's viewpoints is communication. There are many fine books that can help with some of these specific issues. Reading together and then discussing the contents, lovingly and without blame or criticism, can bring about a new understanding of what each partner is feeling and needing. Sexual intimacy is within the reach of all wives and husbands willing to put forth loving involvement.

I have saved some very interesting information for the end of this chapter. I believe that Ellen White wrote it for couples having trouble with sexuality, just as couples do today. She had just written that when Christ reigns in the home, there will be a deep abiding love, "soul will be knit with soul," and there will be harmony. Now she makes a remarkable statement: "Angels of God will be guests in the home, and their holy vigils will hallow the marriage chamber."[3]

I find this exceptionally cheering. This is not a caution or a threat; this is a remarkable promise reminding us that the unitive love experience is a God-created, God-sanctioned, and God-blessed activity. I believe that angels have a much larger role in our lives than we have realized. We too often see them mainly as protectors saving us from plunging off cliffs—well, that too, praise God. "Are they not all ministering spirits sent to serve those who will inherit salvation?" (Heb. 1:14, NIV). That's us! Angels are entrusted with ministering to (attending to, helping, guiding, enriching) our lives in all dimensions, including sexual intimacy. So put out the welcome mat! Invite the angels, ask for their prompting, listen to their cheers.

If after rereading that statement and thinking about it, you are somewhat intimidated, you may want to trace where those feelings come from. You may need to remember again, and again, that sexuality comes from God. It is not a human invention.

Pause Here . . .

Sometime this coming weekend, make plans to carry out this activity. It will take only brief preparation. You will need to have Bibles in which Song of Solomon is written in the form of a dialogue. For instance, in the New International Version the main players are Solomon, the lover, and the Shulammite bride, the beloved. Other lines are attributed to friends.

Since this is going to be a special celebration, you will need two more things: a glass (or goblet) of grape juice for each of you. Now, propped against your bed's headboard (or a comfortable sofa), with drinks within sipping range, you are going to have the pleasure of playing these two lovers' roles.

The husband, of course, will read Solomon's part, the lover. The wife will read the part of the beloved. When you get to the friends' lines, read them in unison. It may look like a long play-reading, but it will not take more than 30-40 minutes unless you stop to do some discussing, which is fine too. I want you to get the full impact of the tenderness and the realness of their love. Remember that this is married love as God planned it. Let yourself be inspired by their words, realizing that they are in your Bible because God wished them to be—for you, for all married lovers.

Recall also that Christ has likened His love for us, His church, to the love He bears for us as His bride. I think it is very significant that He used the marriage relationship as the means of trying to bring to us the full force of His love. His love, which is so pure, so enduring, so exclusive, so tender, so understanding, so cherishing—what can we say but thank You, God! What can we do but strive to model our love after His? What can we pray, but "Fill us with Your love, so that our marriages may be reflected in our love for each other."

---

[1] *Patriarchs and Prophets,* p. 46.
[2] *The Adventist Home,* p. 111.
[3] *Ibid.,* p. 94.

CHAPTER 8

Spiritual Intimacy

We have looked at three important dimensions of intimacy that husbands and wives can share. We will now consider one more intimacy, which undergirds and binds them all together: spiritual intimacy. We could think of the other intimacies horizontally, and the spiritual dimension vertically as the husband and wife together seek a deeper relationship with God. A shared spiritual life strengthens a marriage, and at the same time a good marriage can strengthen the spiritual life of the couple. Ellen White says it this way: "The closer we come to Christ, the nearer we shall be to one another."[1]

First, though, what do we mean by spirituality? How do we define ourselves as spiritual persons? Spirituality is the attention we give our souls. At the core of our being, God has put a longing for companionship with Him. We realize that He wants us, individually, to be one with Him, and we are awed that He accepted death that we might have life (see Mark 10:45). Eugene Peterson reminds us: "None of us provides the content for our own spirituality; it is given to us; Jesus gives it to us."[2] When we accept His gift we are drawn to His life and are eager to learn how He wants us to live in His spirit. We might then say that spirituality is living in the presence of God, in an awareness of God's presence. To be spiritually intimate with our partner, we look for the assurance that she/he also wants to live in His presence.

Historically, God and marriage have been closely intertwined. God instituted it—and gave instructions for its protection and nurture. He performed the first ceremony, giving the principle—"they will become one flesh" (Gen. 2:24, NIV)—still spoken to indicate the ultimate love relationship between partners. Jesus honored marriage by His presence at a festive wedding occasion and by performing His first miracle there. And He pays His church the honor of calling us His bride over whom He will rejoice! (see Isa. 62:4, 5). Marriage has a spiritual ancestry that should be guarded carefully.

Several couples who sought marriage counseling have made this same interesting observation. When they were actively seeking to enhance their spiritual lives, they felt that their relationship flourished. One tearful young wife observed: "As I look back, I can see how we started to drift apart when we no longer made time for prayer and devotions together. We began to see Sabbath as less of an opportunity to renew our spiritual lives and more of a day to sleep in, and just generally do our own thing." And all this time God was wishing that they would long to do "His thing," which was to refresh their spirits with His saints. I think God intended Sabbath to be a great love-in for all His children. "In His own day," writes Ellen White, "He preserves for the family opportunity for communion with Him, with nature, and with one another."[3]

There is real value in joining in *corporate worship* with God's people so that He may "dwell among" them in a special way. He knows the value of gathering together to hear messages planned for spiritual growth. As we listen to the pastor's words, we can be involved in our own "mind chatter" and begin to think of ways that they can be applied to our own situation. If they don't always seem apt, we can think about what might have been more helpful, what else he or she could have emphasized, and discuss it on the way home or at lunch. Even the least inspiring sermons can be a springboard for our thoughts and ideas. If we are informed enough to be critical, we should be informed enough to undertake some thought and study to bring more to the text or topic than we received at the time.

There are a number of ministers in my extended family. I happen to know that sermon preparation is one of their top priorities, and they wrestle with how to present their message to the greatest good. And they pray for God to guide them in that preparation. But sometimes *we* need to be involved in "filling out" a sermon through some research and study after we leave church.

Another avenue of spiritual intimacy is *devotional study*. Some couples prefer to study their Bibles and other devotional materials together the whole time. Other couples handle this time differently. After some minutes of individual study time, they discuss the material with their partner. Being "good" at couples' devotions takes practice, patience, and a willingness to be open to suggestions—undefensively. Some statements in Ellen White's *The Desire of Ages,* my favorite biography of the man Jesus, have helped me understand the way Jesus communicated when He was living on earth. We know He was a sought-after guest, a friend, and a mentor. People wanted to be near Him. His way with people was so sensitive to each situation that He was able to draw them to Himself emotionally, intellectually, and spiritually.

As you read the following excerpts from *The Desire of Ages* regarding the ways He communicated with others, contemplate what it must have been like to be in His presence. I hope you will want to look up the page references and read more about each of these instances in their own context.

"Every glance of the eye, every feature of the countenance, was marked with humility, and expressive of unutterable love" (p. 137).

"His manners were gentle and unassuming" (p. 138).

"The Saviour did not meet argument with argument. . . . With solemn, quiet dignity, He pressed the truth home" (p. 171).

"He was earnest rather than vehement. . . . Love [was] expressed in look and tone. . . . [He had a] sweet, sympathetic spirit that shone out in every look and word" (p. 254).

"He was never rude, never needlessly spoke a severe word, never gave needless pain to a sensitive soul" (p. 353).

"He did not censure human weakness" (p. 353).

His spirit was "calm, even under personal abuse" (p. 353).

"He did not use one unkind or discourteous expression" (p. 515).

He used "gentle touches, . . . loving ministrations" (p. 516).

What a model!

We have talked about devotional study; now let's give some time to *joint devotional prayer.* Learning to pray out loud with and for each other is a strange and intimidating practice for some couples. Many of us are more accustomed to praying quietly, within ourselves. We feel released from inhibitions when we can pray without others listening. With others present we may feel as though we must frame our prayers in an acceptable manner—using correct words and proper phrases and sentences. But the Father to whom we address our prayers (and note I do not say petitions, for I believe we need to think of our devotional prayers more in terms of conversation than a prayer list) loves for us to come to Him. He is listening eagerly, not critically. We were "created for fellowship with God."[4]

Individual prayer will still very much be part of our lives, but now an exciting, new dimension is added. In the prayer life I have shared with my husband for 55 years, the latter years have been even better than the earlier ones, judging by the quality of our praying *and* the amount of pleasure and intimacy it has brought us.

We started, almost without realizing it, by always

reaching for each other's hand when we prayed. Soon we found ourselves doing this at other people's homes, at church—wherever we heard the first words of a prayer. There is something very precious about holding hands with the one you love under any circumstances. It indicates that you feel a connection, a closeness. It says, "I am aware of you. I desire to touch you to validate your being here with me. You are dearer to me than any other person around me. Let me *feel* your presence."

When your hands are enclosed in prayer, it acknowledges the third Party in your relationship, the God who blessed your marriage and continues to sustain your love for each other. At your wedding service you probably were asked to join hands as you made your vows. That in itself says something about the importance of touching at solemn times. Pause a moment to remember reaching out to her/him and the good feeling of that warm (perhaps cold and nervous) hand. Your heartbeat probably quickened and maybe one or both of you exerted a little pressure to send a special signal of your own.

Holding hands during prayer could be considered a mini-vow, reminding you again that your lives are forever joined. It is a wonderful thing to remember, and can't happen too often.

Midway through our marital odyssey, my husband and I added to our prayer repertoire what turned out to be a wonderful blessing to our spiritual/emotional intimacy: embracing in prayer. This consisted of kneeling as we were facing each other so that our bodies were touching close, as we each put our arms around each other. Then cheek-to-cheek we would pray conversationally. Now, when we first heard this described, we were not at all sure how to effect this posture, although anything that included embracing got high marks with us! But very soon we learned how to kneel close enough to each other to be able to "huddle" very quickly and with great enjoyment. It has been some years since we started this, but it is still our favorite way to pray together.

With the passage of years, some aging parts of our bodies have not always felt kindly about the kneeling bit. But assuming the same embracing posture while standing or even sitting is a very good substitute for those days when we recognize time has not stood still where joints are involved!

There have been times when for various reasons we have had to be separated for a few days. It is then that we realize how much we cherish this tradition. We miss these intimate prayers. When I asked my husband if he thought I should include our experience in this chapter, in his characteristically positive manner he said, "Absolutely!" Please try this, expecting a bit of reticence and timidity at the onset, but also expecting a rich reward for being "young" (flexible) enough to try something different to enhance your relationship.

Spiritual intimacy is nurtured by an active prayer life, which in turn imparts a feeling of togetherness in other areas of life. When a relationship has been penetrated by the Spirit of Christ, new avenues, new ways of showing love for each other, open up. One dark-eyed bride of many decades said, "We never knew how much we loved each other, nor how many ways there were to demonstrate it until Christ became our regular prayer partner."

The spirituality I am referring to here is not simply "being on the books" of church membership. It does not mean being able to explain prophecies, holding church offices, sacrificial giving, or even regular church attendance—as important as each of those things may be. Rather, the spirituality intended here extends to and enriches the practices mentioned above, and includes the most kind, the most forbearing, the most understanding and loving way of life brought right into the heart of the marriage. The good news is that God is love, and that love is available to our relationships.

Not only does God exhort husbands and wives to love each other, He makes very clear just what love is made of. Through Paul's inspired "definition" of love (1 Cor. 13:4-7), we know what we can expect when love is present in a marriage relationship. Love will manifest itself by being patient, kind, unselfish, and protective. It will be courteous, optimistic, and slow to anger. It also has a blessedly poor memory of past wrongs.

That could be an intimidating list if we had to come up with those love qualities on our own. But love is not something we can of ourselves generate; it is "heaven-made" and available for the asking, freely and in unlimited quantities. You can't find a better deal than that. I for one am glad that Paul operationalized the concept of love so well and so succinctly. It is an awesome literary truism.

I would like to suggest one more means of enhancing spiritual intimacy: *reaching out to others* with the intent of helping them to experience the same joy as you do in your spiritual lives. There are many ways of doing this, including what I call "heavy-duty witnessing." This might include giving Bible studies, distributing literature on a regular basis, assisting your pastor with evangelistic projects—things of that type. My husband and I have done each of these, and we would be hard put to decide which was the most enjoyable and rewarding. Some of them were "scary" when we first undertook them, but the very process of working through our inexperience—and sometimes our reluctance—brought us a new dimension of togetherness. Our delights when things were going well, our concern when they weren't, laughing together at the humorous things that often accompany new pursuits, discussing new plans—all drew us together.

But I am also thinking of the less formal ways of reaching out: welcoming new members with a visit or a meal invitation, caring for those in our church family—single parents, teens whose parents are not churchgoers, students away from their home church, those ill or with long-term disabilities, elderly persons without children living near, newly married or newly divorced persons, those from homes with embarrassing problems, people who can no longer drive and who would love a drive to a park or into the country, and so on. From experience, I can absolutely guarantee that reaching out by a phone call, a written note, or a visit will enhance your spiritual intimacy.

The desire to have a relationship with Christ and the ability to seek and carry out that purpose are from the same Source as are the desire and ability to seek and carry out a relationship with our spouse. The power to effectuate both of these relationships is the One who created us. He knows our weaknesses and our strengths—who better can we turn to as we seek to bring spiritual intimacy into the heart of our relationship? This promise is worth remembering: "Hearts that are filled with the love of Christ can never get very far apart."[5]

Spirituality and Sexual Experience

In 1980 a woman's nonconservative magazine, *Redbook,* conducted a survey of its readers. An exhaustive questionnaire asked about sexual attitudes and practices—and about religion as well. Since religion has often been cited as one of the main reasons for problems of sexual enjoyment, one survey result surprised many. Women who perceived themselves to be deeply religious turned out to be among those who enjoyed their sexuality the most, and were most satisfied.

Well, why not? These women consider sexuality to be God's plan for their bodies. The qualities of love have been divinely defined for them, and they have God's counsel on conducting successful relationships throughout the Bible. They are assured that God wants their happiness, and they can appropriately make their marital sexual relationship a matter of study and prayer. All the ingredients of a good sexual experience are part of their spiritual orientation. They know that the sexual oneness God intended for maleness and femaleness can indeed be sanctified and, at the same time, a joyous delight.

Let Christians think of this, let them talk of this, let them rejoice with the bride and groom in the Song of Solomon story as they sing their song of love:

"Let us go early to the vineyards
To see if the blossoms have opened
And see if the pomegranates are in bloom,
And there I will give you my love" (S. of Sol. 7:12, 13).

---

[1] *The Adventist Home,* p. 179.
[2] "What's Wrong With Spirituality?" *Christianity Today,* July 13, 1998, p. 53.
[3] *Education,* p. 251.
[4] *Ibid.,* p. 124.
[5] *The Adventist Home,* p. 94.

CHAPTER 9

A Communication Practicum

There are times when a theoretical discussion does not sufficiently provide all the information necessary for a workable knowledge of a matter. Sometimes it needs to be demonstrated. The following skits show the type of marital communication that has a detrimental effect on intimacy.

Read them out loud together, each of you taking appropriate roles. Then discuss how the participants could have averted an unpleasant situation.

Skit 1: Inattention

Andrea is sitting on the couch looking through the mail as she awaits Alex's return from work. She has started to read an article in one of her favorite magazines as he comes in.

ALEX: Oh, hi, honey. What a day! The freeway was like a parking lot. I was late getting to work, and the stacks on my desk kept piling higher all day long.

ANDREA: Hi! *(She continues to read after looking up briefly.)*

ALEX: I can't believe how inefficient people can be at that office. You should have seen the mess we had about the middle of the afternoon.

ANDREA: H'mmm. . . . Oh, really? *(Still reading.)*

ALEX: The supervisor from the head office showed up unexpectedly and asked for some reports I couldn't find.

ANDREA: Uh-huh.

ALEX: After he left, the boss was upset. He said that with business the way it is some of us might have to be laid off. And he seemed to look at me as he left the office in a huff—

ANDREA: What was that last thing you said, honey?

ALEX: Never mind. I think I'll mow the lawn.

This could have been Andrea coming home from work while Alex was watching a playoff game on TV. Without realizing it, the inattentive spouse is saying that the activity he or she is engaged in is more important than what the spouse is saying. If this pattern is repeated with any regularity, neither spouse will feel listened to and will quit trying to break through. Being listened to is a very important—and even precious—experience.

Skit 2: Nothing Is Wrong!

Dinner is over, and Betsy enters the living room after finishing the kitchen cleanup. Ben is reading as she sits down beside him.

BETSY: You've really been quiet tonight.

         (Ben doesn't reply.)

BETSY: You didn't say more than two words all through dinner. Is something wrong?

BEN: Nothing's wrong.

BETSY: Things OK at work?

BEN: Look, I said nothing's wrong. Can't we just leave it there?

BETSY: You know, Ben, some couples talk things over when there is a problem.

BEN: I said *nothing is wrong!*

BETSY: Sure. Nothing is wrong. But it sure would be nice if you could trust me enough to talk about things when something is confusing or eating at you.

BEN: *Look, I—*

BETSY: Yes, I know. Nothing is wrong. *(Gets up to leave.)* I'm going to do some things in the kitchen.

Usually a vehement "Nothing's wrong!" is shorthand for saying, "Plenty is wrong, but I can't discuss it because I'm not good at putting things into words." Or: "You wouldn't understand." Or: "I'm not sure how you could handle the way I feel right now." Or: "I'll handle this alone; men shouldn't have to weigh their wives down with extra problems." Or: "If I do share this with you, it might make me look ineffective/stupid/wimpish."

Good news is easy to respond to appropriately. It takes much more sensitivity, acceptance, empathy, and, yes, goodwill to accept unsettling news in a way that makes the "confider" feel that disclosing the problem was a good decision. We have to "earn" the right to be the confidant of troubling news.

Skit 3: Triteism

Carole and Curt are sitting on the patio after dinner, watching the sun go down, when Curt surprises Carole.

CURT: Do you want to know what happened at the office today?

CAROLE: Of course! I always enjoy hearing about your day.

CURT: Well, you might not enjoy this item. You know the project that I thought was going so well?

(Carole nods appreciatively.)

CURT: You remember how pleased I was with the result? Well, today the boss looked at it and practically gave me the whole thing to do over again.

CAROLE: Oh, that's too bad. . . . But I guess "into each life some rain must fall."

CURT: I just don't know what he wants, Carole. I thought I had incorporated all the things he has always indicated were important. I don't know what to do next—I'm stumped.

CAROLE   *(reaching over and patting his knee):* Well, as they always say, "If at first you don't succeed, try, try again!"

CURT: You know, sometimes I wonder if I'm not out of my league. Maybe I just don't have what it takes for such a competitive, creative workplace. Maybe it's just not me.

CAROLE   *(her voice expressionless):* Curt, just wait and see. "Every cloud has a silver lining."

CURT   *(without enthusiasm):* Thanks a *lot!*

We have to give Carole credit for being eager to listen, but she was not tuned in to Curt's feelings. Instead she seemed to have her own agenda—providing trite, insensitive feedback, a sort of one-size-fits-all solution to situations and problems. Curt was obviously feeling discouraged, put down, and ineffective. He needed Carole to say something like "This must have been a terrible disappointment. I know how hard you have worked on this project. I'm sure your presentation was not 'ordinary.' Your work is always highly lauded by your colleagues. I wish I could wave a magic wand and make the problems go away. But here, let me rub your back for a while and get some of that tension out while we talk some more."

Feeling understood is a wonderful experience. It may not change a situation or mend a broken bone, but it can be emotionally healing. It can give us courage to continue. Ellen White suggests that we should "enter into the feelings" of others. Isn't that a wonderfully expressive phrase? I wonder if one of the reasons that Jesus was so beloved and so welcomed was that He made others feel that He really cared and, of course, He did.

Skit 4: Trivialization

Dorry and David have just returned from an evening with their married child.

DAVID: Do you think there was anything different about the way Jim and Linda acted at dinner tonight?

DORRY: No, I can't say that I do. Why do you ask?

DAVID: It just seemed that Jim was quiet and withdrawn, and I wondered if he was upset with us—or if it was something else.

DORRY: You're just imagining things.

DAVID: No, I don't think so. I felt a difference as soon as we got there.

DORRY: You always take things so seriously.

DAVID: No, I don't *always*. But several times he cut me short when I was talking about their new addition project.

DORRY: You really are a worrier. You analyze every little thing and then get upset about it. Why can't you simply enjoy being with them?

DAVID: When we left, he didn't come to the door—didn't even say goodbye. I wonder if he was upset about my suggesting that he get another bid on the plumbing and wiring. Do you think it sounded as though I was meddling?

DORRY: Oh, stop already! I am not going to listen to any more of this paranoid conversation. Just forget it. Things are fine between us.

DAVID: Well, I only wanted to get your opinion. Obviously you don't want to talk about it, so just forget it.

When a person has a concern, it is not comforting to have it judged as trivial. The message that comes through is that he or she worries about things of little consequence, which may be saying something about his/her rationality. And though that may be possible, it is a rejection of the feelings of the "worrier." Being treated in such a dismissive manner does not contribute to feelings of closeness. Listening, with no more response required than a hug, some gentle pats, and an opportunity to talk about and process the concern, makes everyone feel better.

Skit 5: Inappropriate Humor
Dinnertime conversation

ERIC: Good pie, honey. As good as my mother makes—maybe even better!

ELENA: Speaking of your mother, she called this morning. And even though I tried really hard not to disagree with her, we got into an argument again. As usual, it was about money—more specifically, that I spend too much.

ERIC *(laughing):* You two at it again? Speaking of money reminds me of a good one I heard today. This husband was scolding his wife because one of her checks had been returned, and she said, "Great! What should I buy with it this time?" *(He continues to laugh heartily.)*

ELENA *(remembering the trouble she has with her checking account):* That isn't funny! I'm really serious about having a good relationship with your mother. I wish you would help me figure out how to get along with her better. I think that's part of being a good wife.

ERIC: Hey, did you hear the one about the man

110

who thought he had a great wife and took her out every night to show it—but she always found her way back home! *(Laughs.)*

ELENA: You know her better than I do. I want your advice on how to get along with her.

ERIC: Speaking of advice, Joe asked me for advice at work today. He said it was his wife's birthday. When I asked him what he was getting for her, he said, "Make me an offer!" *(More laughter.)*

ELENA: I wish you would take my problems more seriously. You always make a joke out of everything.

ERIC: Oh, come on, honey! You know what happened to the giraffe when he took himself too seriously—

ELENA: No, and I don't want to know. Just forget it!

It is a well-established fact that humor is a wonderful tension reducer. We sometimes encourage people to "lighten up" and have a refreshing laugh. And laughing has received high marks for contributing to improved health. Seminars have been devoted to demonstrating the positive power of humor on various life systems. So what happened in this skit?

Eric wasn't sensitive to the seriousness Elena was feeling as she asked for help with the problem.

Maybe Eric has gone through this enough times to try to handle it with what he does best—interjecting humor. And it may work for him sometimes. But after two exchanges he could have realized that it wasn't going to work this time.

Elena's comments seem to indicate that she feels this is Eric's routine way of putting off a serious discussion. When he's not comfortable with an emotional sharing of feelings, he resorts to humor, not an unusual maneuver for many people.

Elena may come to him less and less frequently with her concerns. That would be too bad, since *there is no intimacy without disclosure.* Therefore, the intimacy level of their marriage will be negatively affected.

Skit 6: Sympathetic Anger
Conversation during an after-dinner walk

FRED: I'm glad you told me about your good visit with Jenny. She really has been a good friend. Did anyone else call today?

FLORENCE: Well, I wasn't going to mention this one . . . but yes, your aunt called.

FRED: Oh? What did she want?

FLORENCE: She wanted to talk about the Thanksgiving dinner we had with your family.

FRED: Did she have anything specific in mind?

FLORENCE: Yes, she did. As usual, she criticized us because she says we always come late.

She knew it was my fault because you didn't have that problem before you were married.

FRED: She has a short memory. Any other complaints?

FLORENCE: She also said the food I brought was just thrown together, not like the real gourmet cooking your family is famous for. She wouldn't dream of bringing deli potato salad and bakery cookies. I yelled at her, and she yelled back at me. Then she hung up. It was awful!

FRED: That makes me mad! Where does she get off, calling here and insulting you? She has always been a miserable cook. Beans out of a can are better than the baked beans she brought. I have a good notion to call her and give her a piece of my mind.

FLORENCE: No, don't do that. There's no use getting the whole family involved.

FRED: Nope. She's done this once too often. She's always been a troublemaker—

FLORENCE: Please, Fred, don't do that. I'm sorry I even told you. I didn't know it would upset you this much. There's no point in the whole family being mad.

Doesn't Fred get some credit for taking his wife's

side? Well, "sides" don't matter much where anger is involved. Anger is not noted for solving, soothing, or salvaging a situation. Nor is it a good supportive strategy. Who knows how long it will take until the family is righted after this situation?

Speaking of families, we might wonder whether Fred and his aunt have some longstanding conflict that is being deflected into this situation. It really strains intimacy to intrude one generation's problems into another's.

Skit 7: Outdoing

Gwen and Gordon sit down at the breakfast bar.

GORDON: I really had a bad night. I don't know how I'm going to get through the day.

GWEN: I'm sorry, honey. What was wrong?

GORDON: My back is so sore. I just couldn't get comfortable all night long. Every way I turned was pure misery.

GWEN: I know what you mean. I've had times like that. Last month, after we put in the lawn, I had the same trouble with my back.

GORDON: I had to get up and take an aspirin. I should have doubled the dose. *(Groans as he rubs his back.)*

GWEN: Aspirin doesn't even touch *my* pain.

GORDON: It's even hard for me to stand up straight now.

GWEN: It took me weeks to feel comfortable when I stood. And since aspirin upsets my stomach, it's hard to find a pain medication that really works. I guess we just have to realize that. Where are you going?

GORDON: I'll see you after work.

GWEN: Are you leaving already? I was just going to suggest—

GORDON: Never mind.

We might smile at this "painful" one-upmanship. But it can happen in other areas, too. For instance:

RITA: Work was impossible today, right from the beginning—

ROB: Don't talk to me about a bad day. Mine was a disaster!

True, it is sometimes quite comforting to share our misery, and many spouses feel good about being able to listen to their partner's problems. It makes them feel trusted. However, trying to outdo each other's distress is not helpful for either one.

The solution? Take turns. Ladies first? The most patient partner defers? Take your pick.

Skit 8: Interrupting

HELEN: This checkbook record really upsets me, Hank.

HANK: Why? What's the matter?

HELEN: I see that you wrote Ricky a check for
          $200, and that is contrary to everything
          we decided to do.

HANK: Well, I guess I should have—

HELEN: Yes, I guess you *should* have! We talked
          this over with Ricky's parents, and they
          didn't want us to keep underwriting his
          car expenses.

HANK: Just a minute. I had a phone call from
          Ricky, and—

HELEN: So you cooked this up with him without
          telling me about it.

HANK: No, we didn't. If you would quit inter-
          rupting me, I'd—

HELEN: And what about his parents? How do you
          think they feel about this?

HANK: Well, if you will listen for a minute, I'll tell
          you how they feel about it—

HELEN: Sure you will—after you have already
          gone behind their backs. And mine, too!

HANK   *(muttering):* I sure would like to get to
          have *my* say around here.

So what was the rest of the story that poor Hank
was never able to share? It seems that Ricky had been

ill during one pay period at college and was short of money for an insurance payment. After he made satisfactory arrangements to take care of this financial shortage, Ricky checked with his parents, who agreed with his receiving the check from Hank. In fact, Helen also agreed when she heard the whole story.

Hopefully, she learned from this experience not to interrupt before her communicant has completed a line of thought. Doing so often averts unnecessary misunderstandings and accusations. It certainly would have in this situation.

Skit 9: Just Like Me

While watching the evening news, Irv and Inez are talking during a commercial break.

IRV: You look upset tonight, honey. Anything wrong?

INEZ: I was talking to Eunice this afternoon, and I guess it kind of upset me. She was here while I was baby-sitting little Ryan today. She thinks I'm spoiling him, and she gave a lot of advice on how to handle him. It just doesn't seem comfortable to use her techniques.

IRV: Have you let her get on your nerves again? I'll tell you what I'd do: I'd just tell her I didn't need her help and to leave me alone.

INEZ: I couldn't do that, Irv. She's an old friend, and she means well.

IRV: She might mean well, but I don't like it when she upsets you. If I were you, I'd remind her that I didn't need her help. In a nice way, of course.

INEZ: There must be a better way to handle it. I'll think about it.

IRV: My way works for me every time. Just tell it like it is. That's the best way.

INEZ: I know you think I should handle things the way you do, but being that forthright is just not for me. Sometimes I feel that if I don't do things *your* way you don't think I'm an OK person.

IRV: The philosophy behind *my* way is that when you become more aggressive, it changes the balance and—well, I know it's right because I've read a lot about it.

INEZ: I have some laundry to fold . . .

IRV: Well, if I were you, I'd think about taking my advice seriously.

Inez is feeling the way many persons do when someone else's way is held out as the best—and only—way to do anything. It not only promotes a feeling of "inferiority by contrast," but it can cause resentment. People who profess to know it all are difficult to *want* to be with, not to mention to emulate.

Skit 10: Criticizing

Jed has just come back from a shopping task.

JUDY: Well, did you get your money back?

JED: No, I didn't, and I wish I had never listened to you and gone back to the store.

JUDY: Why? What happened?

JED: The clerk was really rude. She said that the sweater didn't even come from that store, and if it did, it must have been a special consignment sale, and I couldn't return it for a refund.

JUDY: Are you sure you were listening right, or were you just not paying much attention, as you often do?

JED: Of course I was listening!

JUDY: Well, then, did you ask for the supervisor?

JED: No, I didn't, and I don't plan to. *You* can take it back if you want to.

JUDY: You are so passive! You just let people walk all over you. You need to stand your ground.

JED: I hate shopping! And I especially hate returning things.

JUDY: You're just too easy on people. Like at the restaurant last week when they brought the wrong order. Most people would have asked for their order to be done over, but not you! You went ahead and ate something you didn't like rather than ask.

JED: The spaghetti wasn't so bad without tomato sauce.

JUDY: I'm beginning to wonder if you'll *ever* learn to take the bull by the horns.

JED: What's that got to do with my sweater? You know, I'm beginning to like it better and better. I think I'll just get a pair of slacks to match.

JUDY: Purple slacks! You *are* hopeless. I only wish you would get some backbone.

We can imagine how Jed feels after this exchange. If Judy's criticism is directed toward changing him, it will certainly fall far from the mark. A more assertive partner often finds it difficult to understand someone who is reluctant to speak up. Not everyone needs to be a "speaker-upper." Maybe one marriage doesn't need two of them.

If Judy would let Jed be Jed, they could have a happy and intimate life. Jed probably has many other good qualities that more than make up for what Judy perceives as a deficit.

Sometimes it's important for husbands and wives to recall the list of wonderful attributes the other has—out loud. One of those times is when one is feeling critical of the other. Very few behaviors are changed for the better through criticism.

Skit 11: Preaching

Kara and Ken are getting ready for bed on a Friday evening.

KARA: Be sure to set the alarm tonight, Ken. Last week we were late for Sabbath school. I like to be on time for Al's rousing song service.

KEN: Look, you go ahead tomorrow. I don't think I'll go to church.

KARA: Not go to church? What's the matter?

KEN: Nothing's wrong. I'm going to stay home and listen to the United Nations discussion on the Middle East crisis. This is pretty serious stuff.

KARA: Why, I never heard of such a thing. We've never allowed secular things to interfere with our Sabbath attendance.

KEN: Well, this time it will.

KARA: Aren't you getting a little careless about your spiritual commitment?

KEN: Oh, don't get carried away!

KARA: No, seriously! I've noticed other little signs that have concerned me, and I'm wondering about your spiritual direction.

KEN: Now that you bring it up, I'm in the middle of doing a lot of reevaluation of the church—and religion in general. I'd rather not discuss it at this point.

KARA: Well, I'm glad this came up right now. I've been looking up some references on becoming lukewarm . . . I have them right here; I think we should go through them together. Paul has some good exhortations. And Ellen White also brings some pertinent light to this topic. Here, let me show you—

KEN: Look, Kara, I really don't want to go into all this right now. Just leave it alone, OK? Don't make a federal case out of my staying home from church one Sabbath.

KARA: But Ken, sometimes you have to get at the little foxes before they spoil the vines.

Recalling your marriage vows will probably not bring a memory of promising to preach to your spouse as a way of securing your marriage, either spiritually or emotionally. Since most partners are concerned about the spiritual tone of their marriage, it's easy to want to be a positive force in that direction. One husband, worn out from dodging the texts and quotations hurled at him in the interest of his achieving "higher ground," finally told his wife to quit being his personal Holy Spirit.

The good news is that our Holy Spirit is alive, well, and active as our comforter, counselor, and exhorter, leading us into all truth. He has had eternities of experience in these roles, so we can trust Him to do what we cannot. There is one thing the Holy Spirit cannot do for your spouse in the way that you can: love in a personal, hands-on way. Let that be the way you express your concerns for each other.

Another option for Kara? "I'm sorry you're not coming. I always enjoy walking into church by your side and greeting our friends. I like standing beside you during the singing and the praying. But I know you love our Lord and His assembly as much as I do and that we'll be together there again soon."

Skit 12: Why?

Laura and Lance are driving to the market.

LAURA: Did I tell you that Jenny called about our missing the picnic last Sunday?

LANCE: That was nice of her to notice.

LAURA: That wasn't it—she wanted to say that she was disappointed in our reliability on the committee. She always manages to make me feel guilty about something. She intimidates me.

LANCE: Why do you feel that way?

LAURA: I don't know—it's just the way she talks.

LANCE: I've always found her to be friendly and pleasant enough.

LAURA: She's probably nicer to you than she is to me. She is to most men.

LANCE: Why would you say a thing like that?

LAURA: She just makes me uncomfortable.

LANCE: You shouldn't feel that way.

LAURA: I guess it's my inferiority complex at work.

LANCE: I don't see how you can get those feelings.

LAURA: It's easy when you feel as I do inside.

LANCE: You'll have to get control of those feelings.

LAURA: Yes, I suppose so, but it's hard for me to feel good about myself.

LANCE: Why do you let yourself feel that way?

LAURA: I don't *know* why I feel that way. *I just do!*

LANCE: Calm down! I was *only* trying to help.

To be called upon to explain our feelings is sometimes seen as threatening. We are usually unaware of what goes into the making of something as complex as our feelings. "Why?" makes us feel as though we must understand, justify, explain, or account for them. This is sometimes difficult even for a professional therapist to do. It doesn't make us feel as though we are being accepted as we are.

Starting a question with Why? is usually not a good idea when we are talking about emotions. There are better ways to demonstrate interest and empathy. Telling someone that they should or should not feel a certain way is really a judgment call. Few of us know *how* we should or should not feel in another person's circumstances. It can be seen as presumptuous that we *think* we do.

Skit 13: Mentoring

Mindy comes home from work and slumps down on the sofa beside Mark.

MINDY: I don't know what kind of day you had, but mine was not so good.

MARK: Really? What happened?

MINDY: You know that the principal and I used to get along so well together. Well, it seems as though he has been avoiding me lately. Today in faculty meeting he ignored any suggestion I made altogether. When we meet in the hall, he hardly recognizes me. He hasn't looked in on my room for days. I hardly feel that I'm part of the team anymore.

MARK: Well, in that case, I think the best thing you can do is walk into his office tomorrow and tell him how you feel.

MINDY: Oh, I *couldn't* do that! It scares me even to
          think of confronting him, sitting behind his
          big desk.

MARK: You simply have to learn to be more as-
          sertive. That's your problem.

MINDY: I know I have a hard time speaking up for
          myself outside the classroom. My family
          has always been quiet-spoken people who
          don't want to make waves.

MARK: I've tried to help you see this many times
          before, honey. You just have to learn.
          You'll never get ahead if you don't learn
          how to take care of yourself in these situa-
          tions. Hey, I just thought of something: I
          saw an announcement in the paper about
          an assertiveness training seminar at a local
          high school's adult program. . . . Here it is
          right here. Let's sign you up for this the first
          thing in the morning.

MINDY: No, no! I've heard about those things—how
          you have to get up in front of other people
          and tell your experiences and do assign-
          ments. That scares me! Just let it go—I'm
          sure things will get better. Maybe it's my
          imagination that the principal is different.

MARK: Well, I wish you'd take my advice. I'm
          only trying to help your career.

Two people marry for various reasons besides love. Among these reasons are companionship, emotional support, sexual fulfillment, and financial benefits. But few, very few, people marry to get a boss, a supervisor, or a mentor. These roles don't seem to be compatible with love and romance. Actually, love and romance flourish best in an egalitarian atmosphere. True, perfect equality is more difficult to maintain, but it must be the best plan because it's the plan God implemented in the Garden of Eden for Adam and Eve—they were created as equals.

This does not mean that husbands or wives cannot be helpful in the decision-making process. See the next skit!

Skit 14: Decision-making

Nora comes home with big news!

NORA: I really have big news tonight, and I really need your help in making a decision!

NICK: What's all the excitement about?

NORA: My boss wants to promote me to the position of accounts manager. Can you believe it?

NICK: Yes, I can! That's wonderful. Congratulations! *(Hugs and kisses all around.)* So what's the big decision?

NORA: Nick, that is a tremendous responsibility, and I've never done that kind of thing before. I'm not sure I should attempt it.

NICK: Why, that's a real compliment, Nora! Your boss has great confidence in you, and you deserve it. You've done a great job there and made some innovative changes.

NORA: I wish I felt as much confidence in myself . . .

NICK: Is that why you're hesitating?

NORA: I think so. If I felt I could really do a good job, I'd have no problem accepting.

NICK: It seems to me that's the way it was in the past, Nora. When you came to new situations you were unsure about, you were generally cautious in your response. But after you accepted, you found you could manage splendidly. I think everyone has some feelings of insecurity in a new situation. But your track record shows that you have come through every time.

NORA: That's true. I'm glad you reminded me of that. Yes, I think I'll accept. Thanks for your vote of confidence, Nick. I'm so glad we're a pair!

NICK: You're sure right about that! Hey, let's leave the leftovers for one more day and I'll take you out to dinner. Let's celebrate the new accounts manager!

This is a demonstration of a helpful response. First, Nick warmly congratulates Nora. Then he reminds her of past patterns of insecurity, but recalls how well she has done in her work roles. To top it off, he makes it a time of celebration in a way most women warmly appreciate—a dinner invitation! I'm so glad Nora didn't insist on cleaning out the refrigerator or plead weariness, aren't you? This is a much better ending—and one to remember.

CHAPTER 10

In Conclusion . . .

We have looked at intimacy from different angles. We have examined it as experienced by some of our friends in Scripture. We have noted the developmental steps on the intimacy continuum that lead two persons who have never met to become a bride and groom pledging their lives in total intimacy—marriage. You have followed yourselves through that process. And we have looked at four intimacies that sustain and nurture a marriage relationship.

Here we will end our exploration with two topics. The first will bring to view some of the roadblocks to intimacy, for, as stated earlier, intimacy is not automatic. It must be protected, and it must be nurtured. Which brings us to the second topic: a "prescription" for keeping your relationships alive and healthy.

Roadblocks to Intimacy

A roadblock is generally provided to keep us out of danger—to keep us from problems ahead. Sometimes they seem like a nuisance, and often we chafe at them and would rather avoid them to save time and inconvenience. What we discover is that in not heeding the signs, we can cause delays and greater problems for ourselves. Occasionally we may get away with not paying attention to the cautions—which may make it easier to ignore the advice the next time. But in the end we find that it would have been to our advantage to heed the roadblocks at their first appearance.

Roadblock cautions to protect marital intimacy may work the same way. If they are consistently and repeatedly ignored, your relationship will be endangered—if not immediately, certainly over time. These roadblocks are not covered in order of importance, and some may be issues you have already worked through. Good for you! However, you will probably recognize others that have come to haunt you every now and then, perhaps all too often. Each of them, when not heeded, have at one time or another been the source of severe marital problems, even separation.

1. Insufficient time together. "You don't know our schedule," you say? That's true, but I imagine it is a very full one. But let's do away with the idea that it will grow easier at any stage of marriage. Learn now to carve out time together and to use your time to the best advantage. Let's consider some of the things you now spend time on, and then decide if you are investing minutes and hours where it "pays off" best.

Here are some activities that, timewise, should be nonnegotiable: working, sleeping, personal care, health routines, home care, recreation, and time together—just the two of you. Yet several of these are often cheated. For instance, the neglect of health routines—exercise, sufficient rest, proper nutrition—can be the catalyst for impatience, lack of understanding, and even conflict, which could negatively affect your relationship.

Sometimes "recreation" is negotiated right off the schedule. But not only does "all work and no play make Jack a dull boy"; it makes Jack's marriage a dull marriage. And a dull marriage is at risk. Couples sometimes feel that if they don't have time to play tennis every day, or go to weekly concerts or other ambitious projects, they simply can't work recreation into their busy schedules. Here are some "mini-recreations" that don't take much time or money: walking a couple blocks each evening, playing Scrabble (or another game), listening to a favorite CD while cuddling on the sofa, doing a few brisk exercises together, reading an interesting book out loud, cooking or baking together—now think of your own.

2. Too much time spent on nonbonding activities. Probably the main offender here is television, which can creep into your schedule almost imperceptibly. Even when content is nonobjectionable, moments turn into minutes and then hours. Sometime, just for the sake of interest, jot down on a pad on top of the television set (put there for that purpose) all the minutes spent on television in one week's watching. At the end of the week, try to recall the things that *really* nurtured your relationship in ways important to both of you. You may decide that this inanimate object in your family room—or wherever—is a prime-time thief of intimacy. Spending precious hours getting to know the characters on the sitcoms better than you do your own spouse is a poor commentary on priorities. I'm not suggesting that you consign your set to the next yard sale, though some who have done that are pleased with the results. Others have decided to sharply restrict what they watch—and the time they allow for watching.

There are many things on the "tube" that have value. But they usually are onetime specials that have long-term interest, not weekly appointments—which are easy to get "hooked" on. Let me suggest that television time should be prescheduled, rather than turning on the set randomly (and sometimes automatically). This prevents shopping and cruising, which can all too often grab you and rob you of time with your spouse. I am awaiting a news item about someone suing their television set or computer for "alienation of affection."

Couples have to decide how many social activities they should be involved in without sabotaging their own times together. Having a friendship network is as important for couples as it is for individuals. However, an undue amount of time spent with friends can rob your "couple" time. Your marital relationship is your *prime* relationship—never forget that.

Many couples have set for themselves a goal of having one "date" together a week. Some have told me that this has revitalized their relationship, and that whenever they get too involved to carry through with this plan, their feelings of closeness are affected. We are not talking about expensive, noteworthy ventures. A date for a Dairy Queen some hot summer's evening, a walk around the neighborhood, a drive in the park, a museum prowl—all have been lauded by couples. Having a plan, trading suggestions, and keeping that time slot open spells "I love you."

3. A noticeable decrease in the "early attentions." Loving touches, words, and looks that say "you are special" are truly important in the nurturing of a relationship. This need takes very little time per incident: It doesn't take any longer to say "I love to see you sitting there reading—it makes me feel so lucky" than to walk through a room. How long does it take to stop and ruffle the hair (his, not hers) or nibble an ear (either's), or to write a quick note and pass it to your spouse at a most unexpected moment, or to pucker your lips as you look at your spouse across the room, or to reach for his/her hand while you are silently driving along? Have you ever noticed that driving-in-silence syndrome? Don't let it go to waste—it's good discussion time. With a little deliberate practice you will find ways and occasions to make yourself very beloved to the other.

4. Any rough physical acts. Shoving, cuffing, pushing, slapping, hitting, and pinching are plainly "out of bounds" and can wreak havoc on intimate relationships. I mention this because a surprising number of married people think that this is acceptable behavior—if it doesn't cause bruises and lumps. Love expresses itself in gentleness, kindness, and respect. Harsh behaviors can too easily get out of hand, especially during times of tension, insecurity, or low self-esteem. Violence is almost always a learned behavior. When a spouse comes from a home where physical violence or abuse was present, it can too easily invade their own home.

At the very first sign of any of the above behaviors (which are more often male behaviors), there should be a *red alert,* which will include an immediate appointment with a counselor. If one spouse rejects the idea of seeing a counselor, the other should make plans to go alone—it is that important.

5. *Other road bumps.* We won't cover them all in detail, but these road bumps are quite easy to recognize and, if consistently repeated, should also receive attention: unwarranted jealousy and possessiveness, carelessness with personal hygiene and physical appeal, unreal or unmet expectations of sexual intimacy, excessive blame for problems, not taking personal responsibility, deteriorating communication skills, and leaving God out of the relationship. When couples conscientiously make their marriages a subject of study and discussion, they can bring about a true revitalization of their relationship. Now let's take a look at the prescription I promised.

Daily Minimum Requirements for an Intimate Marriage

On your vitamin bottle there is usually information on the benefits you will receive from each supplement. It is based on a "daily minimum requirement." You then decide what is best for you as you seek to maintain a healthy body. We can also prescribe a set of "daily minimums" to keep an intimate marriage alive and healthy.

I began to distribute this list to couples who expressed a desire to be "closer." (Note: None of these demonstrations of affection are intended as a prelude to intercourse, although at times they may be. They are freestanding expressions of closeness to be "administered" any time during the day.)

- ❧ Offer at least one sincere expression of appreciation.
- ❧ Say "I love you" in ways that please your spouse.
- ❧ Share a feeling or idea that you wouldn't share with anyone else.
- ❧ Make an appropriate, appreciative response when your spouse shares with you.
- ❧ Initiate a full body hug every time you separate or meet again. Full body hugs are so intimate that they belong in the marriage repertoire. Bear hugs and side-by-side hugs are also great.

Pause Here . . .

Each of you secretly choose a day in which you count the times that you hug each other (when you're out of bed). Don't let your spouse know what day you have chosen—this might cause a deliberate change in hug counts. Then before disclosing your separate total hug counts, ask your mate to give her/his estimate of how many hugs took place on the designated day.

If you are an average couple, the wife will have a lower count and the husband the higher estimate—which often means that she would have liked more, while he may be satisfied with hugs as they are. Then tell each other about how many hugs you would like every day. Laugh and have fun with it—laughing and hugging go well together.

❧ Kiss your spouse in at least two different ways. What does *that* mean? Just this:

Couples sometimes get into the habit of using the standard "one-size-fits-all kiss" after a few years of marriage and forget all about the lingering, romantic kisses of courtship days. There are several kinds of kisses: the kind you give old Aunt Mabel when she visits; kisses that brush the forehead, cheeks, or lips; standard "goodbye" kisses; the kind you give while your eyes are watching television or reading; long, passionate kisses; and those in between. I hope it wasn't its "forbiddenness" that made kissing so enticing when you were discovering each other. Now you don't even have to sneak one. Enjoy! Make an art of it!

❧ Consider the following ways to demonstrate affection. (Remember, we are not talking exclusively about the kind of touching that is a prelude to intercourse.)

- stroking
- cuddling
- patting
- snuggling
- rubbing gently
- caressing
- hand-holding
- tracing with fingers on the other's skin
- cheek-to-cheeking

How many of these do you get into each day's repertoire? If you seldom engage in more than five, you may want to consider stepping up your "little attentions." Ask your spouse how she/he feels about that.

Marks of an Intimate Marriage

So how can we evaluate whether we have an intimate marriage or not? The following information, gathered from several theorists, is most significant. Read it dispassionately, if you can. It isn't intended to cause feelings of inadequacy but to provide a goal toward which both partners can strive as you continue your "life study."

1. Just being together is deeply satisfying. This is not to say that you don't want or need a network of friends, but you won't need them to feel alive and interested. The TV won't give the only evidence of life in your home, nor will the computer be your main source of interaction. Sometimes just being in the same room, on the same couch, gives you profound contentment as you occasionally exchange words, touch, wink, or smile. It feels *good*. It feels *together*.

2. You generally agree on important lifestyle issues that could affect your relationship. But when you do disagree, your first impulse is to listen, not to contradict or argue.

3. You can discuss things with a sense of security that your remarks and ideas will not be used against you later to embarrass, belittle, or unkindly tease you.

4. When you realize that some issues need further discussion and clarification, you set aside a time to talk about them together, rather than let them gather baggage.

5. You feel comfortable in revealing weak-

nesses and strengths to each other and expect support and cheers, as appropriate.

6. You have fun together and take time for recreation and laughter.

7. You attach importance to expressions of love, giving extra attention to special days and occasions. Tradition-making is important to both of you.

8. You can allow differences without being threatened, which means you might disagree on a political candidate, a church policy, a child-rearing method. You can disagree without being dogmatic. Negotiating and compromising are prime tools in your marriage.

9. You feel free to accept or postpone sexual invitations without fearing pouting or withdrawal.

10. You feel comfortable discussing your spiritual lives together and enjoy praying out loud with each other.

One final but vital reminder from Ellen White: "The plant of love must be carefully nourished, else it will die."[*]

Thank you for allowing me to guide your thinking about your relationship. My prayer throughout this writing has been that it would deepen your intimacy with each other in ways that God intended. In the process I found myself moved to do the same in my own marriage. My husband has remarked that it has been a good experience for him, too, and has reinforced his desire to strengthen our love—which he was already very good at.

So we both invite you to join with us in the marriage doxology: "Praise God From Whom All Marital Intimacies Flow!"

---

* *The Adventist Home,* pp. 195, 196.